Guillaume le Clerc composed *Fe:* early thirteenth century. Nothin apart from his name and his Frei of his possible identity can be found in the second appendix to this translation). But Guillaume was surely a man of literary interests, as the influence of the Arthurian romances of Chrétien de Troyes and his successors can be clearly perceived in *Fergus*, although Guillaume succeeds in adapting this popular matter to his own purpose. The result is an enthralling tale in which Guillaume builds on his audience's familiarity with the characters and conventions of Chrétien's romances, but nonetheless achieves a new dimension in the genre by adding his own special blend of parody and wit, and a unique Scottish setting for his hero's adventures.

D. D. R. Owen was Professor of French in the University of St Andrews, 1972–88, and taught there from 1951. He studied at the Universities of Nottingham and Cambridge, where he obtained his PhD in 1955, and in Paris at the Sorbonne and the Collège de France. Among his books are *The Evolution of the Grail Legend*, *The Vision of Hell*, *Noble Lovers*, *William the Lion 1143–1214* and a translation of *The Song of Roland*. Joint editor, with R. C. Johnston, of *Fabliaux* and *Two Old French Gauvain Romances*, he also edited *Arthurian Romance: Seven Essays* and published chapters on Arthurian Romance and Chrétien de Troyes in *European Writers: The Middle Ages and the Renaissance*. He was General Editor of the journal *Forum for Modern Language Studies*, which he founded in 1965. He also translated Chrétien de Troyes's Arthurian romances.

FERGUS OF GALLOWAY
Knight of King Arthur

GUILLAUME LE CLERC

Translated, with an introduction and notes,
by D. D. R. Owen
Professor of French, University of St Andrews, 1972–88

JOHN DONALD

First published in 1991 by J. M. Dent & Sons Ltd
This edition published in Great Britain in 2018 by
John Donald, an imprint of Birlinn Ltd

West Newington House
10 Newington Road
Edinburgh
EH9 1QS

www.birlinn.co.uk

ISBN: 978 1 910900 23 9

British Library Cataloguing-in-Publication Data
A catalogue record for this book is available on
request from the British Library

This translation, with introduction and notes, was first published in
Arthurian Literature VIII, ed. Richard Barber (D. S. Brewer, 1989)

Typeset by Biblichor Ltd, Edinburgh, UK
Printed and bound in Britain by TJ International, Padstow, Cornwall

CONTENTS

Introduction	vii
Notes on the Translation	xvii
Select Bibliography	xix
FERGUS OF GALLOWAY	I
Notes	III
Appendix A: *Fergus* and the Continuations	127
Appendix B: Guillaume le Clerc: William Malveisin	159

INTRODUCTION

Guillaume le Clerc's *Fergus* is a masterpiece of its kind. Misjudged in the past as being no more than a competent reworking of material largely purloined from Chrétien de Troyes, it has been passed over with a shrug by most scholars along with other 'second-phase' romances modestly exploiting the vogue of their day for Arthurian adventures. Its literary qualities having mainly gone unrecognised, such interest as has been shown has focused on its unique Scottish setting. However, far from being a mere erratic curiosity, it can claim a place of distinction in the mainstream of French romance as it evolved in the high Middle Ages, broadening its smile in anticipation of the richer comedy of Ariosto and Cervantes.

Guillaume certainly knew Chrétien's works intimately and also those of two of Chrétien's successors who had attempted to bring his last unfinished romance to a conclusion. This familiarity did not, I suspect, breed contempt in Guillaume for either the individual works or the genre, but rather inspired him to play a teasing literary game with both their themes and the conventions they had established, and hence with the expectations of his own audience. A desire for novelty as well as a sense of fun probably guided him in his task. For, though we can know nothing certain of him apart from his name and French (probably north-eastern) origins, we see him as a man of literary interests and talents, anxious to experiment in this relatively new genre (the most reasonable time to place his work seems in the late twelfth or early thirteenth century, within about a generation of Chrétien). It would have been folly for him to try to compete with the

narrative skills, technical dexterity and general sophistication
that had won Chrétien his enviable reputation. Instead, he would
indulge his own taste for parody. Rather than create brand-new
tales of love and adventure, he would make his public's acquaintance with the master and his Continuators work for him by using
some of the familiar characters and situations, but in a craftily
twisted form that would produce, along with an entertaining
story-line, a totally new dimension of witty comment for the
delight of the initiated.

The modern reader unconversant with Guillaume's models
will miss a good deal of the subtlety of *Fergus* that would have
been relished by the more literate among his contemporaries. In
the notes to my translation some information is given on the
most significant of the source elements; and in Appendix A I
have provided renderings of the main episodes in the
Continuations travestied by Guillaume. It will be seen that while
the adventures of Perceval as related by Chrétien and his second
Continuator provided his basic inspiration, he also dipped freely
into *Erec et Enide*, *Cligés*, *Yvain* and the First Continuation.

Although the alerted reader of *Fergus* will recognise many
more or less distorted echoes of these works, the spirit of
Guillaume's romance is personal to him. One detects in the
Continuations little evidence of underlying significance or *sens*,
to use Chrétien's term. They offer simply a succession of adventures, misadventures, marvels and mystifications calculated more
to grip the attention than to provoke thought. Chrétien, on the
other hand, enjoyed confronting his characters with moral or
emotional dilemmas, thus posing for his public riddles to which
he was careful not to supply the answers, questions of social
duty or propriety such as would provide matter for debate in the
cultured circles for which he was composing. The relationship
and interplay of love and chivalry was at the heart of these
matters, the practice of *courtoisie* or civilised social behaviour in
the courtly world of his day the ideal implied in his romances.
He did not lack a sense of humour, as is particularly evident in

Lancelot or the Gawain adventures in the *Conte du Graal* (significantly, perhaps, the part of Chrétien's corpus least used by Guillaume); but it was a humour without bitterness, inviting tolerant smiles rather than sardonic laughter, and often based on close human observation.

Guillaume le Clerc's favourite technique was to reverse elements in his models. When he does this to purely narrative elements, he may simply produce a variant narrative situation, often touched by incongruity or a tone of burlesque, as when a fair maiden plying a comb becomes for him a hairy hag wielding a scythe. If, however, his model has a more serious dimension (for instance an exemplary purpose), his reversal of elements may appear to be a deliberate subversion of that dimension. An example is his use at the beginning of his romance of Chrétien's opening scene in *Yvain*. There one finds an illustration of ideal *courtoisie* as knights gather with the ladies in the castle halls to tell tales or discuss affairs of the heart. By contrast, Guillaume dispenses with the ladies and has instead Gawain drawing Yvain aside for an intimate conversation. For someone familiar with the original the impression is one of conscious misogyny, even of critical comment on the practice of courtly philandering. The change here has not, as it happens, produced a situation that is humorous in itself; so the question is raised as to whether Guillaume, through his manipulations, was offering his privileged public at least some measure of personal comment. The matter is left for the individual reader (or more likely, in Guillaume's age, listener) to decide; but it remains a fascinating area to explore.

One does have the feeling that some of the conventions of the romance were alien to Guillaume's nature. His treatment of the sentimental theme is far from orthodox, as foreshadowed by that opening scene. There is something essentially matter-of-fact in his make-up; and such elements of the supernatural as he does use are likely to be undercut a little. With the rough-and-tumble of challenge and insult he is thoroughly at home, adept as he is at verbal deflation and endowed with a barbed wit and a ready fund of black humour. The character that emerges from his work is, then, that of a sharp-minded realist, and the absurdities that pack his plot are produced tongue-in-cheek. He even turns his back on idealism in the locations selected for the action of the romance. Fergus does not travel through the vague landscape typical of these Arthurian tales, in which a few names of Celtic origin or pure fantasy suffice to give an exotic flavour. It is no accident that Guillaume's story shows the greatest geographical precision of any Arthurian romance and that the places on Fergus' itinerary can still be visited in the course of a short tour of southern Scotland. This is why it is often suggested that Guillaume must himself have lived in the region.

At the time when *Fergus* was composed, lowland Scotland was by no means unknown territory for Continental Frenchmen. Having earlier been occupied by the Anglo-Saxons, it had long been subjected to Anglo-Norman dominance in social and cultural as well as political matters, and the records are full of the names of settlers of French origin, some having come directly from their home regions, others having moved north from England. Links with the Continent were maintained through marriages among the nobility, political and ecclesiastical affairs, and general commerce. Indeed, by Guillaume's day the foundations had already been laid of the 'auld alliance' between Scotland and France. But an exception must be made of Galloway, whose population, of solid Celtic stock, had a reputation for barbarity, and whose rulers, including the historic Fergus (d. 1161), were often a thorn in the side for the Scottish kings. As for Argyll and the Western Isles, they still owed firmer allegiance to the kingdom of Norway than to that of Scotland. In the middle of the twelfth century Glasgow had been sacked by Somerled, the partly Norse Lord of the Isles, who seems to appear in our romance as Soumillet, the hero's uncouth father (the real Fergus of Galloway was in fact related to Somerled, but only distantly).

Against this historical background, the suggestion that Guillaume was composing for a Scottish patron is not in itself unreasonable. Alan of Galloway, great-grandson of the historical Fergus, was proposed as a possible patron by Ernst Martin and later by M. Dominica Legge; and he might appear a promising candidate until one reflects that he would scarcely have felt flattered by Guillaume's presentation of his domain as a back-of-beyond region lorded over by a rustic commoner. Similar doubts are raised by Beate Schmolke-Hasselmann's suggestion that the romance has a core of serious propaganda in the context of the Baliols' designs on the Scottish throne for their family. Guillaume in any case offers no words of dedication or address beyond wishing joy to those who hear his story. The text lacks clear evidence that it was intended as any kind of 'ancestral romance'; and the search for a patron has proved of doubtful value.

What if *Fergus* is approached from a more literary angle? This can be done by starting from the premise that Guillaume's initial idea was to write a skit on Chrétien and his followers. He would pattern his hero on one of Chrétien's characters: and what better model than Perceval? Not only had his career been left in mid-course by both Chrétien and the Second Continuator, but the notion of a brash simpleton coming to terms with the courtly Arthurian world lent itself to humorous and ironic development. So Guillaume's decision to have a 'neo-Perceval' as his hero is understandable. Perceval had emerged from the desolate Welsh forest: what appropriate homeland could be found for his fellow-novice? Galloway is an obvious answer in view of that region's reputation, of which Guillaume could have been reminded by lines found in some copies of the *Conte du Graal*. There it is characterised as:

> Une terre molt felenesse
> Et si i a gent molt perverse.[1]
> [*A very evil land with very perverse people.*]

A few years earlier the chronicler Jordan Fantosme had been even more explicit:

> La pute gent, ke Damnedeu maldie,
> Les Gavelens, ki d'aveir unt envie,
> E li Escot qui sunt en Albanie
> Ne portent fei a Deu, le fiz Marie:
> Brisent mustiers e funt grant roberie.
> (*Chronicle*, ll. 684–88)

> [*That miserable race, on whom be
> God's curse, the Gallovidians, who
> covet wealth, and the Scots who dwell
> north of the Forth have no faith in
> God, the son of Mary: they destroy
> churches and indulge in wholesale robbery.*][2]

It can be seen that Guillaume might have come naturally to the choice of a Scottish setting for his work, even without having personal connections with the country. As for the name of his hero, he could hardly do better than borrow that of Fergus, the most powerful and celebrated ruler of Galloway in the twelfth century. The name could, of course, have been found first and itself have determined the location – a possible, if less likely, explanation. But in neither case is Guillaume's residence in Scotland a necessary assumption: he could have obtained the limited information he required from some informant or written itinerary or other record.

This is the view I tended to favour until a new line of enquiry was opened for me as described in Appendix B, to which I refer the interested reader. The discovery that the heroine and one or two further characters have likely historical prototypes who were almost certainly contemporaries of the poet now suggests to me that he was composing in the very heartland of the romance, which may in fact be something of a genial *roman à clef*. My search for a potential author with the right qualifications has produced as prime suspect a most unlikely figure: William Malveisin, a one-time royal clerk who rose to be Bishop of Glasgow and finally of St Andrews.

I can do no more than produce my evidence, well aware that difficulties still remain. For instance, what we can discover about the dissemination of *Fergus* suggests that knowledge of it was restricted to the Continent, although insular copies may have fallen prey to the ravages of time. Works from the Anglo-Norman area did often find their way to the north-eastern region of France, which might explain the linguistic colouring of the two surviving manuscripts (there is also a Dutch version, *Ferguut*, preserved in a fourteenth-century copy). The influence of *Fergus* on later French literature is also on texts from the same general area. It certainly left its mark on the hybrid epic *Huon de Bordeaux*, very probably on the second-rate romance of *Hunbaut* and, more significantly, on the charming *chantefable*, *Aucassin et Nicolette*. By contrast, no trace has come to light of any influence on the English literature of the Middle Ages.

Since then it has been unjustly neglected. Guillaume le Clerc, whoever he may have been, was an able poet as well as storyteller, a deft manipulator of the traditional octosyllabic line, who recognised cliché for what it was and largely avoided it or used it for his own irreverent ends. *Fergus* is, then, a lively and well-told tale; but it is more than that. It offers excellent examples of a type of parodic humour, based on the witty reversal of model situations, which prospered in the thirteenth century, perhaps most characteristically in the bourgeois milieu of north-eastern France. To some degree *Fergus* may have been influential in refining this brand of humour as it found its most delightful expression in *Aucassin et Nicolette*. Apart from its own considerable qualities, it holds for the student of literature the further interest that it looks through contemporary eyes at some of the most popular and seminal works of the French Middle Ages. Parody is comment, but oblique and open to differing interpretations. What is Guillaume's own attitude to the genre of the romance, to the individual texts, and to the various elements within them? His provocative work must speak for itself.

Notes to the Introduction

1 Mss *C, P, S, U*: *see* Hilka's edition, variants and notes to l. 6602.
2 *Jordan Fantosme's Chronicle*, edited and translated by R. C. Johnston. Compare *Fergus*, ll. 196–99:

> Mais cil del païs sont molt niche,
> Que ja n'enterront en mostier;
> Pas ne lor calt de Diu proier,
> Tant sont niches et bestïaus.

NOTES ON THE TRANSLATION

Fergus is preserved in two thirteenth-century manuscripts, Chantilly 472 (= A) and the perhaps later Paris, Bibliothèque Nationale, f. fr. 1553 (= P). Both contain numerous scribal errors; but on the whole A seems more reliable (P shows some expansion) and was chosen by both Ernst Martin and Wilson Frescoln as the base for their editions. For my translation I have worked primarily from the Frescoln text, but have resorted from time to time to Martin or to variant readings from P where the sense seemed to require it. My punctuation also departs, quite radically on occasion, from Frescoln's; otherwise my aim has been to provide an acceptably literal rendering such as may be used by students in conjunction with the text and variants he has provided.

Guillaume composed in the octosyllabic rhymed couplets standard for the romance and as familiar to his public as is prose to today's reader of novels. He handled his verse with skill, though simply as the conventional medium for telling a story, rarely seeking particular 'poetic' effects or embellishment. But like any good story-teller, he varied his tone as the situation required, ranging between the more or less formal style of narrative and description and the pungent exchanges of heated dialogue, at which he excelled. It is this variation of tone, not the rhythms of the verse, that I have tried to catch in my rendering. One particular problem in the translation of Old French writers is their frequent and sometimes apparently gratuitous switching of tense between past and present. I have in the main followed Guillaume's practice in this, but have avoided frequent or abrupt changes such as would shock the modern ear.

Paragraph divisions are my own, the line numbers are those of the Frescoln edition of *Fergus*. Asterisks in the text indicate lines, individual passages, or longer sections commented on in the Notes. They are placed at the beginning of sections, or at the end of passages for which closing lines are given (see p. 111).

SELECT BIBLIOGRAPHY

Texts used or cited

The Acts of William I King of Scots, 1165–1214, ed. G. W. S. Barrow (*Regesta Regum Scottorum*, Vol. II), Edinburgh, 1971.

Aucassin et Nicolette, ed. Mario Roques, Paris (CFMA), 1936.

La Chanson de Roland, ed. Joseph Bédier, Paris, 1921 etc.

Chrétien de Troyes:

Christian von Troyes, *Sämtliche Werke*, ed. Wendelin Foerster, 5 vols., Halle, 1884–99, 1932.

Erec et Enide, ed. Foerster, *S. W.*, III, 1890; ed. Mario Roques, Paris (CFMA), 1952.

Cligés, ed. Foerster, *S. W.*, I, 1884; ed. Alexandre Micha, Paris (CFMA), 1957.

Lancelot (Le Chevalier de la Charrette), ed. Foerster, *S. W.*, IV, 1899; ed. Mario Roques, Paris (CFMA), 1958.

Yvain (Le Chevalier au Lion), ed. Foerster, *S. W.*, II, 1899; ed. Mario Roques, Paris (CFMA), 1964.

Le Conte du Graal (Roman de Perceval), ed. Alfons Hilka in *S. W.*, ed. Foerster, V, 1932; ed. William Roach, Genève/Lille (TLF), 2nd edn. 1959; ed. Félix Lecoy, Paris (CFMA), 2 vols., 1972–5.

[Unless otherwise stated, my references are to Roach's edition of *Perceval* and to Foerster's editions of the other romances.]

The Continuations of the Old French Perceval of Chrétien de Troyes, ed. William Roach (Vol. II with Robert Ivy), 5 vols., Philadelphia, 1949–83: Vols I–III *The First Continuation* [= C. I]; Vol. IV *The Second Continuation* [= C. II].

Guillaume le Clerc:

Le Roman des aventures de Fregus, ed. Francisque Michel, Edinburgh (Abbotsford Club), 1842 (from MS *P*).

Fergus, ed. Ernst Martin, Halle, 1872.

The Romance of Fergus, ed. Wilson Frescoln, Philadelphia, 1983.

Ferguut, ed. E. Rombauts, N. de Paepe and M. J. M. de Hahn, Culemborg, 1976.

Hunbaut, ed. Jakob Stürzinger and Hermann Breuer, Dresden, 1914.

Huon de Bordeaux, ed. Pierre Ruelle, Bruxelles, 1960.

Jordan Fantosme's Chronicle, ed. with translation by R. C. Johnston, Oxford, 1981.

Le Turpin français dit le Turpin I, ed. Ronald N. Walpole, Toronto, 1985.

Translation

Chrétien de Troyes, *Arthurian Romances*, translated by D. D. R. Owen, London (Everyman's Library), 1987.

Studies

Arthurian Literature in the Middle Ages, ed. R. S. Loomis, Oxford, 1959 (see pp. 377–9 for Alexandre Micha on *Fergus*).

Ash, Marinell, *The Administration of the Diocese of St Andrews 1202–1328* (unpublished Ph.D. thesis for the University of Newcastle upon Tyne), 1972.

Barrow, G. W. S., *The Anglo-Norman Era in Scottish History*, Oxford, 1980.

Brugger, Ernst, 'Huon de Bordeaux and Fergus', *Modern Language Notes* 20 (1925), 158–75.

—— ' "Pellande", "Galvoie", and "Arragoce" in the Romance of Fergus' in *A Miscellany of Studies in Romance Languages and Literatures presented to Leon E. Kastner*, ed. Mary Williams and James A. de Rothschild, Cambridge, 1932, pp. 94–107.

Duncan, A. A. M., *Scotland: The Making of the Kingdoms* (Edinburgh History of Scotland Vol. 1), Edinburgh, 1975.

Flutre, Louis-Fernand, *Table des noms propres avec toutes leurs variantes figurant dans les romans du moyen âge écrits en français ou en provençal*, Poitiers, 1962.

Freeman, Michelle A., '*Fergus*: Parody and the Arthurian Tradition', *French Forum* 8 (1983), 197–215.

Greenberg, Joan, 'Guillaume le Clerc and Alan of Galloway', *Publications of the Modern Language Association of America* 66 (1951), 524–33.

Jordan, Leo, 'Zum altfranzösischen Fergusroman', *Zeitschrift für Romanische Philologie* 43 (1923), 154–86.

Legge, M. Dominica, 'Some Notes on the *Roman de Fergus*', *Transactions of the Dumfriesshire and Galloway Natural History & Antiquarian Society*, 3rd series, 27 (1950), 163–72.

—— 'Sur la genèse du *Roman de Fergus*' in *Mélanges de linguistique romane et de philologie médiévale offerts à M. Maurice Delbouille*, Gembloux, 1964, Vol. II, pp. 399–408.

Marquardt, Wilhelm, *Der Einfluss Kristians von Troyes auf den Roman 'Fergus' des Guillaume le Clerc*, Göttingen, 1906.

Owen, D. D. R., 'Chrétien, *Fergus, Aucassin et Nicolette* and the Comedy of Reversal' in *Chrétien de Troyes and the Troubadours: Essays in memory of the late Leslie Topsfield*, Cambridge (St Catharine's College), 1984, pp. 186–94.

—— 'The Craft of Guillaume le Clerc's *Fergus*' in *The Craft of Fiction: Essays in Medieval Poetics*, ed. Leigh A. Arrathoon, Rochester, Mich., 1984, pp. 47–81.

—— 'The Craft of *Fergus*: Supplementary Notes', *French Studies Bulletin* 25 (1987–8), 1–5.

—— *William the Lion 1143–1214: Kingship and Culture*, East Linton, 1997.

Paul, Sir James Balfour, ed. *The Scots Peerage*, Edinburgh, 1904–14.

Ritchie, R. L. Graeme, *The Normans in Scotland*, Edinburgh, 1954.

Schlauch, Margaret, 'The Historical Background of *Fergus and Galiene*', *Publications of the Modern Language Association of America* 44 (1929), 360–76.

Schmolke-Hasselmann, Beate, *Der arthurische Versroman von Chrétien bis Froissart*, Tübingen (Beihefte zur *Zeitschrift für Romanische Philologie*, Vol. 177), 1980.

—— 'Le Roman de *Fergus*: technique narrative et intention politique' in *An Arthurian Tapestry: Essays in memory of Lewis Thorpe*, ed. Kenneth Varty, University of Glasgow, 1981, pp. 342–53.

Southworth, Marie-José, *Étude comparée de quatre romans médiévaux*, Paris, 1973.

Stringer, K. J., *Earl David of Huntingdon, 1152–1219: A Study in Anglo-Saxon History*, Edinburgh, 1985.

Watt, D. E. R., *A Biographical Dictionary of Scottish Graduates to A.D. 1410*, Oxford, 1977.

Webster, J. M., *Dunfermline Abbey*, Dunfermline, 1948.

West, G. D., *An Index of Proper Names in French Arthurian Verse Romances 1150–1300*, Toronto, 1969.

FERGUS OF GALLOWAY

It was on the feast of Saint John that the king held regal court at Cardigan. Many were the courtly knights there, whom I could easily name if I wished to take the trouble. For according to the story as I heard it told, my lord Gawain was present along with his very dear companion (that was my lord Yvain, who was never found wanting) and Lancelot, and Perceval who strove so arduously for the Grail. Erec was there, and Sagremor, and the auburn-haired Kay, and many another whose names I cannot give because I have not learnt them. When they had dined, they took their ease in the halls, recounting their deeds and the stern adventures that had befallen many of them on numerous occasions. My lord Gawain had taken the hand of a companion of his, namely Yvain, for whom he showed a love as great as ever was seen: the mutual affection of Achilles and Patroclus was at no time greater than that of these two companions. They sat side by side at some distance from the others, chatting of this and that.

35   While they were talking thus, discussing whatever they pleased and oblivious to all else, the king suddenly came upon them unawares. Noticing him, my lord Gawain at once jumped to his feet, exclaiming: 'Welcome, sire! Pray sit here, if you please.'* – 'On no account! For I have a quite different proposition for you. Have your horses saddled, as I've a mind to set out straight away! Loafing around is not to my taste: I wish to go hunting in the Forest of Gorriende by Carlisle. There's a white stag there I want to hunt down if I can.* If I find it in open country, it will be caught, unless it shows a great turn of speed. I want my order carried out; so come along, nephew, jump to it!' – 'Just as you

wish, sire,' replies my lord Gawain to the king: 'It's not for me to go against you.'

59   At once the squires spring to make ready their equipment, putting saddles on the steeds, loading the pack-horses with chests, saddling the palfreys: the gear was speedily prepared. In short, the king mounts. In all the world there was no man more worthy or who looked more like an emperor. Joyfully the king and his company leave the town. The prudent lord Gawain rode at the right hand of the queen, who, for the summer heat, had put on an ermine mantle trimmed all round with sable that reached to the ground: there was no such mantle in the whole of England or Scotland or Ireland.* On they ride until they find the white stag grazing on a heath close by a lofty mountain.

81   When the king saw it, he was delighted. He braced himself in the stirrups, and, overjoyed, called to all his huntsmen, pointing out to them the white stag. Straightway the hounds were unleashed, and, as the forest rang with the sound of the horn, they made a mighty din and clamour. When the stag hears this, it bounds off at speed. The hounds give enthusiastic tongue, the huntsmen are jubilant, and the king spurs after them. From then right to mid-afternoon they hunted the white stag headlong until they reached the bank of a deep, fast-running river: no broader one in the whole world flowed as swiftly. The stag ran straight up to it, and plunged into the roaring water. But to its great misfortune, a wide bridge stood there, across which the king passed with my lord Gawain following. The rest vied with each other in their eagerness to cross the bridge, only to find the stag already out of the water and dashing more than a bowshot ahead of them through a valley.

111   The huntsmen gather their hounds together, then urge them on to the sound of their horns. The dogs catch the stag's scent as it runs through the wooded countryside, and full of glee they bay fiercely: it would have been music to your ears! In its terror, the stag had no thought of stopping. On it goes through a valley without pause. The king has sworn his oath not to abandon the

chase until he has the stag taken, come what may; and there is no baron who does not consider him better than his word. Then, calling together all his nobles, the king told them that whoever should be responsible for taking the white stag would have his golden cup. Then you could have seen worthy barons charging after it, digging in their spurs! The stag has no thought of stopping, but instead goes fleeing through the vale at top speed as if possessed by the fear of death. On through the valley it goes and then, with jaws agape, enters the Forest of Jedburgh. It almost stuns itself against the oak trees, it is so exhausted. In a thicket it takes cover; and there it stays, panting and thrashing about, with scarcely any breath left in its body.

145   Here now comes Perceval, astride a very fine horse that he seized from the Scarlet Knight.* Looking into the thicket, he noticed the stag that had taken cover there. He at once brandished his spear, intending to strike the stag with it. But it was not yet ready to die, so it breaks cover from the thicket. Wanting no further delay, Perceval goes in pursuit of the stag, which runs off at full stretch, being now somewhat refreshed although already greatly fatigued. The king and all his huntsmen were distressed as never before not to be able to catch it. Then there is general talk of giving up and abandoning the entire hunt. Hearing it, the king threatens that anyone who quits the chase will never again have cause to rejoice. At that they returned to tracking the stag, which tears off, bounding over the moors and running like the wind. But the king is very disconsolate, and his whole company with him, to find the stag not waiting for him but already ahead by a distance of two good leagues and even more. Never in their entire lives would they lay hold of the white stag: rather, the king's promise would be broken, were it not for Perceval the Welshman, who presses on hard after it, still digging in his spurs and refusing to give up yet.

182   Without pausing it passes through the whole Lammermuir district before entering the very extensive Forest of Glasgow. The stag never halted in any woodland, meadow or heath, but sped

on to Ayr, the home of fair women, than whom none are more
beautiful in all the world. Through this region the stag passes;
and Perceval continues to follow it with raised lance over hills
and through valleys until it has come to Galloway, a richly
endowed land. But the folk who live there are very ignorant, for
they will never enter a church: they are so stupid and bestial that
they are not concerned with praying to God.*

200   There Perceval comes up with the stag, but without any
companion save his hound, which often gives tongue in the
stag's pursuit. It was already so close to it that it had just seized
it by the hamstring. The stag leapt into a swamp; but the hound
keeps a tight grip on it, drags it closer and presses home its
attack. Then the stag gives a great cry and sinks in completely.
The hound tugs and bites and thrusts until it has its jaws and
chin quite covered in blood. With a cry, the stag stops breathing
and sinks: now it can drink, if it is thirsty! The water has
entered its body, for it took in a great deal when its mouth was
wide open. Nevertheless it gets out of the water, thinking it can
then make off. But the hound comes in front of it, grabs it by
the nose and pulls hard. The stag dives into the waters of the
pool. It has drunk so much of the cold water that its stomach is
distended and tight; and unable to stand this, its heart fails.
Then it goes floating away on the water. Just see the hound
swimming there, pushing and pulling at it until it has guided it
to the bank!

233   Here now comes Perceval spurring up. He saw the stag lying
quite dead and was very amazed, you may be sure. He set his
horn to his lips and on it gave a long blast, for he was very much
better at that than any of Arthur's companions. The king, still
riding on, clearly hears and is quite convinced that Perceval has
taken the stag. 'Quickly now, my worthy lords!' says he. 'Press on
with all speed, and we'll go to help Perceval. He has done nobly
to catch the stag by himself: I've heard him sound his horn for
the capture.'* They all spur headlong on, passing by a rock and
then a long stretch of forest.

252   At the deep ford beside a thorn-bush they found Perceval on foot having dried off his hound and rubbing its head with his bare hand. Seeing him, the king greets him as his close friend. Perceval returns his greeting with the words: 'Sire, dismount, if you will, and rest; for I swear by my own right hand that this is a suitable place for you to spend the night. And night, I fancy, is drawing on.' – 'You're right,' says King Arthur: 'an excellent suggestion it seems to me.' Then they all dismount together and put up pavilions and tents. It was a fine, tranquil evening, and they passed the night there most happily and with great pleasure, eating and drinking copiously and going to bed when it suited them. Then Perceval had his reward of the gilded cup for taking the white stag and winning the highest acclaim of them all. His reputation was greatly enhanced because he immediately presented the cup to my lord Gawain: that was considered by no means boorish of him.* That night they rested there until it was broad daylight.

283   In the morning when the king wakes, he dresses, putting on his clothes and making himself ready, then asks for water for washing. And the person charged with fetching it brings it in a pair of gilded bowls that had been carried in a chest. The king washed his hands and mouth and bathed his eyes with the water, then ordered his tent to be struck. This is done without delay in obedience to the king's command. After that you might have seen all those tents taken down and dismantled together, then loaded up by the squires, who do not overlook the white stag in the loading, but have it carried away with them: King Arthur, who prized it greatly, has it transported by pack-horse. Then they ride at speed and without a halt towards Carlisle.

303   On the road out of Galloway, in a castle down a valley, lived a peasant of Pelande very close to the Irish Sea. He had his dwelling splendidly situated on a great rock, encircled by clay and wattle walls. The hill was topped by a tower that was not made of granite or limestone: its wall was built high of earth, with ramparts and battlements.* The peasant was very well off

to have such a handsome home by the sea. If he looked out, he could see for thirty leagues all around. Nobody inside could feel threatened by any maker of siege equipment or from any assault, the rock being high and massive. Without a word of a lie, the peasant governed and held in his possession the whole of the country, which had been his for a very long time; and nobody could take it from him. The peasant's name was Soumillet.* On account of his remarkable wealth he took a wife of very noble rank and by her had three most handsome sons of fine physique, well built and tall. Had they been a king's sons, they would have looked the part well, I think, and might easily have been knights. And each day when it grew light, the peasant, rough countryman that he was, would send one or two of them to look after the sheep in the mountains, where he had large tracts of land. The third would go ploughing dressed in a short, shaggy jerkin roughly made from lambskins, and with a pair of rawhide shoes on his feet. Such was the work they were engaged in every day.

345   The king passed that way; and you may be sure he took a long look at the fortress and castle, which was of excellent construction. The shaped rock pleased him greatly. There, by a causeway at a bend in the road, one of the rich peasant Soumillet's ploughs was working that day. Two young men were attending it: one was his eldest son, the other a hired ploughman. The youths were ploughing there when they saw the king pass by and his whole company with him. They would rather have been in Pavia than there at that moment! Neither of them knew where to run in the woods to be safe, convinced as they then were that these people would capture them. Had they dared, they would have made off; but they lacked the courage to move or take a single step forward.* Then the company passed by; and nobody paid any attention to them, nor was a single word addressed to either of them. This gave the two young ploughboys more confidence. Following the procession went a squire driving a big pack-horse laden with silver vessels. He was going behind the company because the

horse was lame in one foot; so the lad was travelling more than a full league in the rear.

381   Seeing him, the peasant's son abandoned where it lay the plough he was holding. In his hand he gripped a club that he carried with him when ploughing; for it was the custom in Galloway to carry weapons while at the harrow or plough. Along a road he came running as fast as his legs would carry him, and very politely he took hold of the squire's bridle and said to him: 'My dear good brother, in God's name tell me without hiding anything who these knights are who are passing this way.' – 'That's King Arthur, my good friend, and with him his knights with whom he has waged his wars and conquered all his lands, so that he rules the realm as emperor.' – 'Tell me too, my friend and good brother, if they really belong to him, those men I've seen with my own eyes keeping so close beside him.' The squire replied: 'Friend, don't think I'm spinning you a story, but those people you saw riding close to the king belong to the Round Table* and are his counsellors in his sovereign chamber.' – 'By my faith,' says he, 'these are grand people good King Arthur is taking with him, and never did any prince have more. I've heard a lot about him and tales of the valiant deeds performed by the lords of his court. So help me God, I want to join this really civilised company of his, come what may. So I'll go to court to serve him, if he deigns to keep me there, and I shall be his counsellor.' – 'You'll do well,' says the squire; and with that he leaves, with no more words exchanged.

426   Impatient to get to his father, the peasant's son waited there no longer, but turned his attention elsewhere and went back to his plough that was supposed to be tilling the fields. He unhitches everything, horses and oxen, not leaving so much as a horse or mare, then removes the ploughshare and coulter. The lad with him did not know why he was doing this and was utterly dumbfounded. The young man, who would have liked to be already at court, is in a great hurry and dashes off at breakneck speed, not waiting for his companion in his very great concern to follow

quickly after the company. On he goes until he gets so extremely
hot that he is quite dripping with sweat and almost passes out.
Never for a moment did he stop running before he came rushing
up to the castle where his father was. Promptly he flings to the
ground the iron tools he is carrying on his shoulders.

452   Hearing him, the peasant looks across and sees his son back
from the fields. He says to him: 'What's happened to you, son?
Let's have no lies! Why have you unhitched everything?' And he
replies without hesitation, giving him a full account of the king
and his company; and then, raising his voice, he cries: 'Father,
for God's sake give me arms and fit me out with them, and I'll go
to serve the king at court, whatever becomes of me! I'll not be
put off from going there, not for any man or for the whole Roman
empire, come what may.' The peasant hears him and runs at him
with a massive stick in his hand. With it he would have given him
a great blow and knocked him to the ground, had he not been
restrained. But his noble wife jumped forward and, seizing her
husband by the arms, held him still for a long time; otherwise, it
seems to me, her son would have had his brains knocked out
there and then.

478   At that he begins his scurrilous talk, quite appropriate to a
peasant: 'Son of a whore! Where do you get the idea of asking to
be given arms? It's your job to look after oxen and cows like your
brothers, who go out in the fields every day dressed in sheep-
skins.' – 'Really, husband, by Saint Mungo,'* says the lady, 'you're
wrong there! You have no one to vouch for the shameful thing
you've imputed to me. I don't think I can be accused of whoring.
There's no man from here to the sea against whom, if he wanted
to examine me on that score, I'd not find an immediate defence
without any hesitation. And regarding this young man, let me
tell you that you shouldn't be surprised if he's set on a life of
prowess, for he has many fine knights in his family – on my side!
So it's my belief he is taking after them. And if you want my
advice, you'll not make any difficulty about him setting off. He's
the oldest* of our sons, and we have two grown-up ones left. Let

this one go into service to gain merit and reputation; then those two will stay with us and do our work. This one is good-looking and has a noble air about him. He'll never find himself in the position of being thought anything but handsome; and he may well earn a high reputation.'

513   Having listened to everything his wife has said, the peasant realises full well that he has spoken foolishly; so he repents and, swallowing his pride, begs the lady to forgive him and pardon the very grave wrong he had done her. 'I'll do as you wish,' says he. – 'Husband, I don't want to be angry with you if I can help it. I don't wish to hear another word about it. But just you give the young man arms!' – 'Very gladly,' says Soumillet, 'since that's what you want.' Seeing a serving-lad in front of him, he told him to bring at once his arms, which had been stored away for thirty-two years and more. The lad promptly jumped up at his master's bidding and opened a chest, from which he took a suit of armour such as I can well describe to you. The hauberk was every bit as scarlet as the sun rising in the region of Ethiopia, but not with red paint or brazil-wood pigment – of that you may be sure. No: it was a trifle rusty, although its links were good and strong enough to stop a man getting killed. It had, however, been laid away for a long time without being moved. The helmet was in an equally sorry state, just as seriously rusted all over as the hauberk.*

550   When the young man sees the lad arrive carrying the arms, he would have wished to be already at the gate, armed on his father's horse and having taken leave of his mother. The peasant has no desire to wait any longer; but, having had a great cloth darker than a blackberry spread out in the middle of the hall, he flung down upon it the blood-red armour. Over a pair of white cloth breeches the youth was wearing he laced the iron leggings. The breeches were not old, and they reached down to his feet: he had no other hose on at the time. He took up the hauberk as quickly as he could and lost no time in putting it on his son's back and lacing the helmet over it. Then he girt on him a sword that was short but very broad. After that a plump, fresh horse was brought

for him. And rest assured that never did any count or king or emperor have one that was better for carrying a knight, or two in full armour if need be; for once it felt a load on its back, it would gallop off like the wind. You may know too for a fact that it is the way of many horses in that country that they run more swiftly over quaking bog than any man could go on foot.*

586 The young man's heart thrilled to see the horse arrive. He goes to seize it by the reins and leaps briskly into the saddle without using the stirrup;* nor had he put on any spurs. The men of the youth's native land always carry a knotted scourge, and he carries one as well. Now here comes a lad bringing him a smoke-blackened lance and an old shield, which he hung at his neck. The lance he gripped in his right fist and his shield with his left. He proceeds to ask for six javelins (you can tell he was simple, because had he shown plain sense, he would just have taken his lance, as is customary).* They are fetched for him, and he takes them and hangs them from the back of the saddle-bow. He then asked for his axe, which was brought for him directly; and that he hung from his saddle-bow, secured by a thong.

611 Once he was well equipped to his own liking, it is no wonder if he was happy. His mother ran to hug him and kissed him more than a hundred times; and then the young man took his leave of the household and his father. His mother, however, displayed her very deep grief, not expecting ever to see him again; and as a matter of fact she never did in her entire life.* Thus she wails and cries aloud like a woman racked with sorrow. Her son, though, has his mind set on other things. Just as soon as he can he descends the steps from the hall, with his mother and all the others in tears.

628 Off he goes, lance in rest, on the horse, which bears him rapidly away. He leaves through the fortress gate and, riding along a grassy road, retraces the way he had come, with his eye on the horses' tracks. He continued by hill and dale until he entered a forest. There he came to a fork in the road; and he did not know which way to take and saw no passer-by to tell him

the route or give him any directions. The youth is in a quandary, for he has lost track of the company he was following. He looks behind him and sees four robbers approaching at breakneck spread, fully armed and with their helmets laced, and shouting to him: 'You scoundrel, you'll leave behind with us that fine charger and that armour you're wearing, or else you'll pay very dearly!'* When the youth saw them, he was not in the least dismayed, but went forward with a greeting. None of them uttered a single word except for one, who said: 'Sir knight, just you hurry down off that horse, because you'll not get any further with it!'

658   The young man replies at once. 'As God's your witness, friend,' says he, 'show me the right way for me to take to get to Carlisle. I want to go and speak with King Arthur, because I'd like to make his acquaintance and shall also want to advise him like the members of the Round Table.' – 'In the name of the living Devil you will, you son of a whore!' says the robber, 'You'll certainly never see tomorrow, nor this evening, I fancy. I'm well aware that your relatives all met their end unshriven from counselling King Arthur and his company in his great hall. Your journey's considerably shortened: you'll never leave this path here!'

676   You may be sure that the young man was very upset to hear himself threatened. Raising his axe with both hands, he brings it down on the front of the man's nasal, and he fell bleeding and unconscious. In his sprawling fall, his thigh breaks clean in two. The fight is over for that one! When the other three saw their companion on the ground mortally wounded, you can be certain that they vented their bitter grief, and all together they went to strike the youth in the back with their spears. He was unable to dodge, but never moved either of his feet from the stirrups on their account. When the young man felt himself hit, he was filled with nothing but rage. Eager to have his revenge, he takes a sharp javelin and with it strikes one of them full on the chest with such violence that it passed through his body without stopping in it any more than it would have done in a silk cloth. The man fell

dead in the middle of the track. Seeing this, the other two do not trust the youth at all. It is clear to them that he is no friend of theirs. So they took to the road; but he was unable to pursue them: instead he rushes to cut off the heads of the men lying there. He hangs these heads by the beards behind his saddle bow, then rides along a narrow path until he comes back on to the highway on which he had left the company.

713   By daily stages he rode over mountains and through valleys until he came to Carlisle in Wales.* In the halls after dinner that day was King Arthur and with him a thousand and more knights who had suffered many hardships. Then along the streets here comes the young man on a chestnut horse that was worth a good thousand pounds in gold. He did not stop until he reached the great hall, where the king was sitting peacefully, surrounded by his noble company. The naïve youth came directly into that hall where the mighty king was seated and greeted him in courtly fashion. The king said to him, very good-naturedly: 'Welcome, friend! What is your native land, and what do they call you in your country? And what have you come for? Tell me at once!' The young man said: 'I've no wish to avoid disclosing my name to you. I'm called Fergus by those who know me in my land.* I've come a long way to look for you here. On account of your high renown I've left my own region and come here to serve you. If you deign to keep me, I'll be your counsellor along with these other knights I see sitting round you.'

748   Sir Kay, unable to restrain himself, said to him: 'By my faith, lad, you really look the part of a counsellor to a king! A blessing on whoever sent you here! We were completely at a loss. We desperately needed, may God preserve us, this advice that we now have. It's true that God doesn't forget those who always serve Him well. Now, thanks be to Him, He's sent us great and splendid aid! For you seem to be a valiant, courtly knight well trained in arms. Never in any country have I seen one so hand-some or better built. That helmet with the gold shining in it becomes you very well, and so does the shield slung at your neck.

That fine, white lance in your hands suits you even better. The truth is, and far be it from me to lie about it, that you're very good at striking great blows with both lance and sword: you've lopped off many a head that way. What the jester used to say is true: that a knight would arrive here who would go to the Nouquetran, where Merlin passed many a year; and he would take the horn and the wimple hanging from the neck of the gentle lion, then blow the horn three times and afterwards fight with the knight who is as dark as a blackberry. Tell me this instant whether you have the heart for it! If the king took my advice, he would retain you on the understanding that tomorrow, at the crack of dawn, you'll go alone, quite unaccompanied, to the Nouquetran and bring us that wimple and the horn hanging with it. You'll bring back with you the knight vanquished and bloody; and then you'll have properly avenged all those he has beheaded.'*

794   My lord Gawain almost went out of his mind with sorrow to hear Kay's despicable words to the simple-minded young man. He said: 'Sir Kay, it's always said that the mouth is somewhat tainted by the foul poison that infects the heart; and, make no mistake, I'm referring to you. You'd have burst here and now if you hadn't got rid of it. Have you sobered up now? Begin again: you've not said much! By the faith I owe the Holy Spirit, I never saw your equal for insulting and mocking people. You speak more like a base lecher than a knight. That's a most unpleasant habit of yours.' My lord Kay burns with shame but does not dare to let it show for fear of crossing my wise lord Gawain. He hid his anger and kept it to himself: 'Ah, truly I didn't mean any harm with what I said but was simply pulling the young man's leg.'

819   The youth had heard very plainly how Kay had mocked him; and that really put his back up. He glared at him and said: 'By the faith I owe Saint Mungo, if I wouldn't be thought an idiot, sir vassal with the braided hair,* you'd pay very dearly for your gibes at my expense! If you weren't in the king's presence, I'd let fly at you to such effect that I'd slice through all your ribs.' – 'Come

now, good sir,' said the king: 'don't start such a squabble in my
great hall in front of these people! Rest assured that you shall
have such amends made as will quite satisfy you, I think. But tell
me, if you don't mind, where you got those two heads hanging
behind your back.' – 'Sire, I've no wish to lie to you about that.
The day before yesterday four wicked robbers attacked me in the
woods back there, though it wasn't sensible of them, wanting to
have my horse and threatening more besides. By Saint Mungo at
Glasgow, they didn't know me very well: if they had known
anything about me, they would never have assaulted me. They
were as stupid as animals. I lopped the heads off two of them.
Once I'd knocked them to the ground, and the other two had
seen that and spotted that their two companions were dead,
they didn't fancy attacking me. I didn't care to go in pursuit, but
took a path that led me to the main road where I'd stopped
following the tracks. Now I've come here before you. Tell me,
lord king, if I shall be retained as your counsellor on condition
that tomorrow I go to avenge your knights on the Black
Mountain,* whoever may lament over it. And so I'll have the
wimple and horn.'

866   – 'My good young man, may it not please Saint Victor that I
should retain you on these terms! I don't wish you to come to any
harm on my account. You'd be in for trouble if you went to the
Nouquetran, searching on the Black Mountain. I don't advise
either you or anyone else I can see to go looking for that lion.'
The youth says: 'I'll not be put off for any mortal man. I don't
want your seneschal to be thought a liar in the matter: no, I'll be
off at dawn tomorrow, if you're prepared to have me in your
service.' – 'As you please then, friend!' says the good-natured
king, who was able to tell clearly from his appearance that he
came from a good family. Now the young man is more joyful and
jubilant than ever before because King Arthur has thus retained
him in his household. Now nothing he sees displeases him. Then
he approached the king for his leave to go and find quarters in
the town. This was readily granted him by the king, for he had

no doubt that he would be given lodgings within the stronghold; and for that reason he gave him leave.

895   The youth leaves the court, on his face a glad, happy expression, not that of someone plunged in gloom: he thinks himself just as good a man as Roland! He goes riding about the town, but without finding a living soul to speak to him or take him to his house, or there being anyone he could ask. A light rain began to fall, a very fine drizzle; and the water seeped right through his hauberk to his bare skin. With his lance erect he goes up and down the streets like an idiot. In the end he plants the lance under a laurel-tree, leans there in the wind and rain, and begins to doze off.

914   In a room on the upper floor of a house, an attractive, shapely and well-mannered maiden looked down through the window and saw that handsome, well-built young gentleman asleep. Going down as quickly as she could, she approaches him with a greeting and asks him what he is about, on watch there at such an hour. He is not taken aback, but answers the maiden: 'I'm looking for a lodging, my fair one; and if you're happy to do so then put me up, and you'll be doing a good deed. You'll certainly lose nothing through me.' The girl laughed and said: 'I'm afraid, sir, that it's not up to me to give you lodging. My father is the king's chamberlain, and he's the master of this house. No one takes lodging in here. Even so, I'll go so far as to put you up here for the night on condition that my father agrees when he gets back from court. If he shows the least annoyance or displeasure on your account, then you'll do well to go away again: I couldn't take your part if he disapproved of you.' – 'Damsel,' said Fergus, 'I ask no more than that of you tonight: give me lodging until he comes. He'll not blame you for that; and if he should show you the sharp end of his tongue, I'll leave his house and go to look for lodgings somewhere else.' With that he dismounted and walked into the house.

954   Here then is the young man lodged in quarters where, you may be sure, he will be shown much consideration and honour before

he leaves. The girl runs into the bedroom and fetches a very rich
mantle, which she put on the young gentleman once she had had
his armour removed. Then she had his horse installed in a fine,
handsome stable. Having removed its saddle, two grooms rubbed
its back well down. But they are highly alarmed to find the heads
hitched on behind the saddle. They promptly take to their heels
in fright and, running straight up to him, ask him directly what
that is under his cloth. Then he gave them an account of all his
activities since he left his country and a detailed description of
the robbers he had killed. And when the damsel hears him, she
thinks wonderfully highly of him for this, saying it was most
courageous of him to dare wait for the robbers. She orders the
heads to be taken and dumped somewhere out of the way where
they would cause no trouble or alarm.*

985   The young man has fine quarters: never since he was born was
he lodged better, more to his liking or more comfortably, for he
sees nothing that displeases him. Wearing a grey mantle, he took
his seat beside the maiden by the blazing, sparkling fire. He
would have been very handsome had his face not been bruised
from wearing armour; and had he known how to fit himself out
in the English fashion, one could not have found in any land a
knight more handsome than he. Conducting himself in the
manner of his own region, he nevertheless greatly pleases the
beautiful, sensible maiden, who is favourably impressed by his
spirit and physical charm. She could see nothing about him that
did not utterly delight her, apart from the ugly accoutrements he
was wearing: he had on a pair of rawhide shoes, white breeches
and a shaggy jerkin as when he went ploughing, never having
changed his apparel after his father armed him.

1013   They spent a long time in this fashion, speaking of one thing
and another, until it was time for supper. Two handsome serving-lads from Lothian,* who were extremely capable and courtly,
hurried to bring in the water. The young man washes, as does the
girl, who could easily have been a queen. At the meal they sat
together side by side on a rich, grey-brown fabric. Over a white

dining-table was spread a cloth for the two of them alone, the
household and servants eating at another table. I have no wish to
talk at length of the courses, but they had many of them to their
hearts' content. If I did now want to tell the facts about their
dishes, as I could, I should make my matter that much longer and
might spoil the work with it. So I do not want to toil over that,
preferring to concentrate on composing something better, if I am
able to turn my mind to it. I am not keen to put in inferior matter,
but should like to devote myself to a quite different subject.

1039   They sat for a long time over supper until, it seems, the chamberlain returned from court. He sees his daughter and, at her
side, the young man who had been given lodging. Not being used
to that, he was much taken aback. The maiden sitting beside
Fergus jumped up to greet her father, her face flushed. The young
man too, on seeing him, leapt straight to his feet. But her father
tactfully said to them: 'Stay as you are: don't bother to move. I'm
going to sit beside you.' With that they each sat down. The chamberlain was good-hearted, prudent and courtly and well versed
in all customs. He goes to recline next to them and then begins
questioning the young man as to whether he has been given lodging (a highly surprising thing to him), or whether he has been
foolish enough to appropriate quarters and a lodging.

1065   'Not I, sir, so help me God! I'm not like that, good sir!' says
the good-looking youth. 'I've been given lodging on the understanding with your daughter here that if you grant me hospitality,
I shall be put up for the rest of the night, and that if you're
unwilling to do so, I'll go on to look for lodgings somewhere
else.' – 'May it not please God on high,' says the genial chamberlain, 'that my house should be exchanged for another, now that
you've been given lodging. What's more, I'm very grateful to my
daughter and think all the better of her for having taken you in;
and I'm most anxious for her to show you honour. Are you the
man who was at court before the king a little while ago?' –
'Indeed I was, sir, I assure you: never doubt it. But that person
who mocked me today isn't at all in his right mind, I give you my

word on that. He'll pay for it some time when he least expects it. He's extremely foolish and ill-mannered; and I'd very much like you to tell him from me, if you please, to beware of the peasant's son.' Those were the words he spoke to his host.

1096   At that a young gentleman removes both cloth and table for them. After the meal two serving-lads bring them the water; and then, having washed, they asked for the wine. In a silver goblet they were served with good wine, both honeyed and spiced, for of that the host had a plentiful supply. They went to recline on a couch – the chamberlain along with Fergus and the maiden: just those three, as I understand it. There they had a discussion, the three of them, on various matters. The master of the house, a very courtly man, said to the youth: 'My dear good sir, are you a knight yet?' He replied that he thought he was: 'I am a knight, by my head, because the good peasant dubbed me when he sent me to serve at court. And he gave me his good horse (there's none better this side of Galloway) along with a shield, hauberk, lance and helmet as good, I warrant, as any here in your king's realm. I've been dubbed to my liking. If I were armed on my charger, there's no knight in your court who would put a scrap of fear in me so long as I had my axe and six javelins hanging at my saddle.'

1128   It is plain to his host that he is a simpleton, full of monstrously foolish ideas. Drawing towards him, he puts his arm round him with a noble, kindly gesture and says: 'I presume, dear friend, that you would not be averse to kindly granting me a favour I should appreciate. And I would truly like you to know that it will bring you great honour and far greater profit; and you would never arrive in any place where you'd not be held in greater affection for it.' Hearing him talk like this to the effect that, should he grant him such a favour, it must redound to his honour, he is not justified in refusing him – on the contrary, he freely consents that he should do and say what he likes regarding him and all he has, agreeing to everything. 'Now you've replied as I would wish,' said the chamberlain at once with gentlemanly courtesy. 'The granting of this favour will bring you high honour. Tomorrow at morning mass you are to be a newly fledged knight, and you shall have equipment that is richer and more handsome than this. You shall stand as a knight tomorrow before the best king in the world, for he himself with his own hand will gird your sword at your side and give you the accolade as is the custom of this country. Be careful not to look bewildered, but conduct yourself in a courtly, civil fashion, for I shall fit your spurs to your feet myself. That much I shall do for your honour.'

1169   At that Fergus is very distressed, since he is to lose his accoutrements that he brought from his land. Had that favour not been granted, he would not have renewed or changed his equipment for anything. He is left quite glum and disconcerted; yet he did just say: 'By the faith you owe me, my good host, shall I be made a knight twice? Wasn't I then dubbed by Soumillet, the peasant who loved me well?' – 'Good brother, I have no wish to lie to you: nobody can make a knight unless he also is a knight: know that for a fact. And you have pledged me to do as I wish: take care not to break your word, for that would be the height of folly.' When the young man hears and understands that there will be no other outcome, he promises his host everything he has asked of him.*

1193   Thereupon the lord ordered that the beds be prepared for them to retire to rest and sleep; so the attendants hastily made them ready. The youths proceeded to take the rawhide shoes off the young man's feet. The chamberlain, at great pains to give him worthwhile instruction, goes to take him by the right hand and leads him into a bedroom. I fancy I have still to hear tell of a more luxurious one; for, according to the account I have heard, both sun and moon were painted there, and there is no single star you would not have seen in that room.* The man who carried out this work was amazingly expert, bringing everything together in a small space. The room contained a single bed, in which they put Fergus to lie on a sheet of rich brown material as fine as any this side of Thessaly. In no time Fergus was asleep.

1218   The chamberlain left and came straight to his daughter, who was sitting with the others, and said: 'My sweet daughter, when you get up in the morning have some breeches and a shirt ready for the young man. I don't imagine you're so short of them that you don't have a good supply.' – 'I'll have what clothes you wish brought, dear sir, and he shall have them when he gets up tomorrow.' The beds are made, and they retire to them until it grows light the next day.

1231   Early in the morning the chamberlain rose and called his household, his daughter being already up, fully ready and supplied with what he had asked her for. With the maiden, the master of the house came as quickly as he could to the bedroom, going up to the young man and calling him. Fergus rises quickly, and the damsel hands him the splendid clothes, which were of fine quality. These he puts on immediately; so he was dressed and rigged out, complete with hose and shoes laced on. As he left the room he looked most handsome, with a complexion like fine crystal. So radiant was he that you might have expected him to light up the district and entire country:* such was the great beauty bestowed on him by the Lord God who, with deliberate care, had fashioned him with His own hand.

1253   Then he is anxious to get to the court. At once a lad runs up bringing him his charger, though without having been to harness it with all the trappings Fergus had when he arrived. He brought him nothing of this, but left behind everything except his good steed. That Fergus was not willing to change, for it was just to his liking. Straight away he asked his leave of the maiden and took it, as she gladly granted it.

1265   At that, without more ado, Fergus departs with the chamberlain; and they go at once to speak to the king and request arms and equipment. The king had come from church and asked for a chessboard, to play with one of his lords. Before there had been a checkmate, Fergus and his host arrived in court. They dismounted at the foot of the staircase, then climbed it to come before the best king in the world. Fergus strides straight into the middle of the hall. The people sitting there stare hard at him and, seeing how handsome and good-looking he is, murmur a great deal among themselves. They say: 'Never before has Nature formed so handsome a being!'

1284   He hurried through the great hall and came before the king. Putting his hand to the cloak hanging from his neck, he took it off; for his host had taught him that, and he remembered his lesson well. The frank, noble-hearted man remained in just his tunic. He would not have known what to do, had his host not told him to prostrate himself at the king's feet and ask him for arms. The young man was not backward, but promptly knelt down, seized the king by the legs and feet and saluted him; and after that he asked him without delay for equipment appropriate to a knight.

1303   The king looks at Fergus and, seeing him well-mannered, wishes to raise him up. But his response is: 'No more of that! If you don't give me equipment, I'll never budge from here.' The king said to him: 'I shall give you some. But tell me where you come from and what your name is.' – 'Don't you recognise me? I'm the young man who was here yesterday and was mocked by the seneschal. But you may be sure that the way he spoke was not very sensible: I've not forgiven him for the wrong he did me, and he'll pay for it yet. He'd better beware of me!' – 'My friend,' said the king, 'by my faith, don't be so bad tempered! If my lord Kay has done wrong, don't doubt that he'll make you amends for his misdeed to your satisfaction.'

1325   Just then my lord Gawain arrived, holding in his hand a knife, with which he was whittling a small stick. He said to the king, having clearly heard the youth ask him for equipment: 'Listen to me, sire. My lord Kay's in the habit of speaking offensively to all knights, intimates and strangers alike. He has a very rough, sarcastic tongue. But let all that be. It's quite right that you should give the young man arms and a horse. Remember Perceval, of whom Kay deprived you. He took him from you by his hurtful talk, as you well know.* But forgive him this time, and I don't think he'll do it again. Be quick and give arms and gear to the young man, who seems very worthy; for he's been on his knees too long. If it didn't displease him, I should very much like to propose to him that from now on we should be companions, he and I, in all friendship and sincerity.'* – 'Good nephew,' the king replied, 'then I too beg him most urgently to agree.'

1354   Fergus was quick to reply: 'Good sir, I in no way refuse either your friendship or your companionship, and am most willing to be entirely yours to do whatever you wish. But I would first like to have such equipment as is appropriate. After that I'll set off, perhaps, in search of the wimple and horn and will also fight the knight who guards the horn. If I can find him on his look-out hill, either he'll kill me or I him: one of us won't manage to come out of it unscathed. Then, when I've fought the combat, I'll come back and hope to get to know you and make friends: I don't look for any better than yourself.' When my lord Gawain hears that Fergus has no intention of failing to go directly on that dire adventure, he is extremely heavy-hearted, as are all the others. With one accord they curse, execrate and call on the Lord God in Heaven to confound the tongue of Kay the seneschal.

1383   Fergus pays little heed to them, for his heart is kindled by Prowess, and Valour counsels him, saying in his ear that he should go to the fight and take no account of their pity. Thus prompted, he pressed the king insistently to make him by his grace and favour a new knight. The king realises and sees very plainly that no pleading will influence the youth with the fair locks. He calls for a good set of arms for the dubbing of the young gentleman, and is speedily brought the hauberk and steel helmet, with many knights looking on.

1401   On the flagged floor of the great hall sat Fergus, a fine figure. He was not inept at arming himself. First he drew on a pair of leggings of iron chain-mail, after which he took the fine hauberk and put it on his back. The courtly lord Gawain placed the pointed helmet upon his head. Here now comes Perceval the Welshman making his way down the middle of the hall. In his hand Perceval held a sharp sword presented to him by his good host who had given him lodging.* Perceval was no boor: he placed it in the hands of King Arthur, who then girt it on the young man. The chamberlain busies himself with fitting the right spur, and the Knight with the Lion* goes to attach the left one. Never before, I think, was such honour done in the court of any emperor to any knight as to Fergus; and rightly so, noble and of excellent character as he was. And thereafter he was the finest warrior ever born of mother, though I would make exception of Gawain, who never found his equal or was overcome by any man. That is why I would except him. Nevertheless, apart from him, Gawain, there is none better than he.

1435   Fergus is handsomely armed. From the stables they brought for him the charger, a fine steed, but he was not prepared to exchange the one he had brought and which was at the foot of the staircase. A squire quickly goes down and leads his own horse to him. Fergus seizes it by the bridle and, with my lord Yvain holding the stirrup, throws himself onto its back. They bring him a great quartered shield, which he takes and at once hangs at his neck. In his hands they have placed the lance, which was strong and stout as he would wish. Once he was armed on horseback, he would not have been so delighted, I fancy, had anyone given him four cities. He braced himself in the stirrups with such wonderfully fierce pride that he all but burst the good horse on which he was seated.

1458   'God,' said the king on seeing this, 'how my heart may grieve when Kay through his wicked talk has deprived me of such a very valiant young man! It's a mockery and an outrage against me.' The jester sitting by the hearth began to call aloud: 'Don't be dismayed, sire, for no man will be able to stand against his chivalry! In no time you'll see the knight arrive here from the Black Mountain promptly delivering the wimple and horn; and he will make you what amends you wish. But as for the seneschal, you may be sure that the wicked things he was guilty of saying to the young gentleman will bring great harm and disgrace on his head.' My lord Kay goes almost beside himself with rage. Had it not been for the shame he would have incurred, he would have given the jester a sound drubbing and hurled him right into the fire. However, for the shame of it he leaves him on this occasion, not wanting to let his feelings show.*

1483   Fergus thereupon took his leave of the king and the distinguished lords; and first and foremost he asked and took his leave of my gallant lord Gawain, who was as reluctant to grant it as he could be. They repeatedly pray that Jesus Christ may preserve him from all difficulty and let him return to them. Fergus remains there no longer, but sets off with all possible speed.

1495   Fergus departs and journeys on quite alone, and not with his face bowed down: he is like a lion in his pride. One would not find a bolder knight than he in all the world. For the whole day until noon he rides on straight ahead, but without finding any adventure, which annoys him sorely. A little before evening, as he is passing a hill with a look-out post, he raises his head and looks across to see a great, strong castle standing beside a river on which a fleet might have sailed. Turning his horse's head, he goes spurring towards the castle, which was called Liddel.* He is most impatient to get there. Fergus heads straight in that direction and finds a bridge below the gate.

1516   A worthy man, taking his leisure with a very fine falcon on his wrist, was amusing himself on the bridge; and with him was an attractive maiden, to whose creation Nature had devoted her most expert attention. And, assuming it has ever been possible for anyone to describe any maiden so fair and beautiful, I should like now to apply my mind to that for a short time, without being tiresome. I am not acting like those people who go round spreading lies in a way that annoys everybody: you may be sure of that. I shall never tell a lie about her, but will speak the truth as recounted to me. The maiden's name was Galiene. Should one scour all foreign lands, one would in no way be able to find a lady of greater nobility or the source of higher honour. And she it was who was henceforth to suffer for Love, who would have her endure all the usual range of his ills, the sufferings and the bliss with which he pays those in his hire.

1544 Love should be wholly committed to the maiden: it could find no better repository, for she was well and attractively proportioned, with sparkling laughing eyes and brows that were rather brownish and not very big, but on the small side. Her forehead and face were paler than the white lily-flower. But Nature, wanting to devote some care to that, gave them a flush of crimson to enhance the white, so that the world did not hold her equal. Once Nature had added that crimson to the white in her face, she took very great pleasure in looking at her. One could undoubtedly have reflected oneself in her as in a mirror.* You may be certain that you might have sought high and low throughout the world without finding her equal.

1565 She had a shapely mouth as pretty as if adorned with roses. Her teeth, small and completely even, were whiter than ivory or crystal. Her shoulders were a trifle broad, her arms long, her hands tiny but not immoderately so; for Nature's attention to her formation had been so close that she made not the slightest error in it. She had small breasts just like two little apples, and her flanks were graceful and shapely. But I fear I have wasted my words in describing her appearance, for there is nobody who could tell with his lips or conceive in his heart the beauty that Nature was pleased to assemble to make so attractive a body. She was not merely beautiful, but wise as well as fair. Truly, Nature never made her like. All beauty I consider deficient except for that which she possessed.

1590 Galiene was walking to and fro over the bridge with the worthy man, whose locks were white. Heading straight for where the gentleman was disporting himself with the graceful maiden, Fergus gave him a loud greeting in a courtly, polite manner before asking them for lodging. The gentleman did not remain mute, but replied, 'You're very welcome, dear friend. Dismount at once, for you'll certainly have good lodging to your complete satisfaction! Your horse will be very well supplied with hay and oats in here.' Fergus heard him and was not slow to dismount there and then.

1608   With courtly tact the maiden held his stirrups for him. But Fergus was very concerned because, under Nature's guidance, he wished to show her great respect and honour, though he had no training in that other than what was given him by the knight who had sheltered him; but he had not been with him for long. He did nevertheless retain all the good advice he had given him: the remainder came from Nature. Nature teaches the knight that he must honour and revere his host and that so attractive, beautiful maiden; and this he did in all sincerity. He took the maiden by the hand, and she most willingly took his. Here now come two squires running up to take his arms, for they had plainly seen the knight dismount below the bridge. Without waiting, they removed the shield from his neck as well as his other accoutrements. Fergus was left in just a light silk tunic, handsome in body and flanks, large in the shoulder and with fine hands. He had long arms and massive fists. Proud as he was, he wore no cowardly expression.

1640   *The maiden looks at him intently, deriving much pleasure from gazing at his handsome looks and radiant face as well as his bearing. Everything pleased her equally, and more than anything at all she might see in the world. Love notices and keeps his eye on her. He busily prepares and makes ready, then fits a bolt to his crossbow (a crossbow with a windlass, that is). He hits the maiden right in the eye with a gold-tipped bolt, and so hard that he drives it through the eye and fast into the heart. But if anybody accuses me of having said or done anything wrong by claiming that Love shoots with a crossbow and not a long-bow, I shall justify such a belief, for it is worthy of credit. Love makes his bolt pass directly wherever he wishes: armour is useless against it. Love shoots with great force; and no man, in however strong a tower, can withstand his assaults. No one is invulnerable against Love. But at least his missile is such that it does not inflict a mortal wound: the veins of those who suffer its agony are not severed by it. Such is Love and his nature.

1672   That was the anguish and care that overcame the fair maiden and of which she will never be cured; nor will she be free of that

wound for all her living days. On account of her love, the maiden
frequently changes colour; but she dissembles to the best of her
ability so that none of them notices the workings of Love, who is
making these assaults upon her. Joyfully and gaily Fergus crosses
the bridge with his host. He puts over his shoulders a mantle of
fine cloth lined with vair which one of the squires had brought.
The other took charge of the splendid horse and led it straight to
a stable, where there was a good supply of fodder and oats and
whatever a horse needs. Now let the worthy man think of seeing
to Fergus' needs and pleasure, for his horse has every comfort.

1695   The gentleman, a very sensible person, mounts all the steps
together with Fergus and the girl, who kept her face well lowered*
because of her fear that her uncle would look at her and gather
from her colour that she was so utterly in love's sway. But her
uncle notices nothing. They continue right to the paved floor of
the main hall, which was by no means small. They took their
seats on the couches, Fergus beside the maiden. Her great fear
makes her heart flutter, and she does not dare address the one to
whom she has freely surrendered her entire heart and person; nor
did he speak a single word to her. Thus the time it takes to go a
league passed after the starting horn had been sounded for them
before they exchanged a word: he did not know how, and she did
not dare. So they both abstained until supper was prepared for
them and they sat down to it. They had as many as ten courses;
but anyone who described each one would seem like a leg-puller,
and for that reason I have no wish to set about it. For I want to
turn my thoughts elsewhere, if I can apply my mind to the matter.

1726   When they had sat for a long time over their meal, which was
excellent and just as it should be, the serving-lads removed the
tables, which were made entirely of ebony. The gentleman
addressed Fergus, asking and enquiring of him where he was
born and what he is seeking. Fergus told him everything, concealing nothing from him: how King Arthur dubbed him, and how
he was mocked by Kay. After that he told him straight away that
he is on his way to the Nouquetran to take the horn and wimple:

'And if the man who guards it dares resist, then, come what may, I shall not leave there without a fight. If I can vanquish and overcome him, his war will have run its course.'

1745   The gentleman hears and understands plainly that he is full of mettle. But he is very worried by the journey he has undertaken out of bravado. So he said to him: 'My friend, dear brother, the emperor had little love or affection for you, it seems to me, to have sent you to a place from which nobody can return. Everyone has to die there; and so will you, make no mistake, and that will be a tragic shame. But if you were prepared to believe me, you'd put off this expedition for today and tomorrow, and for ever. You've taken up too heavy a burden; and I've heard a proverb to the effect that overloading kills the packhorse: that's why I'm so afraid for you. That knight where you're going is exceedingly wicked and versed in evil. He's cut the heads off more than a thousand men, and don't doubt it. He's such a master of guile and trickery that there's no knight in the world who dares to confront him any more.'

1771   Hearing what his host said, Fergus merely laughed and then replied with some affection: 'My dear good host, there's no turning back. A gale abates without much rain. Let a coward turn to flight; but I'm not one yet. On the contrary, I'll have the wimple and horn. Sir host, don't advise me to carry away my shield with its flowered design as intact as you see it. What would my lord Kay say then? The seneschal would mock me for evermore, and rightly so. I'd rather die than not go there!' When the worthy man hears that he is wasting his time in pleading with the valiant youth, he says to him: 'Don't take what I've said amiss, dear friend. I give you my solemn word that I've said it more for your good than for my own, because if I had my way, you'd never want to go to that place.'

1795   They conversed together in this way until, once the beds were prepared, they retired to rest. But the bright-faced maiden was unable to sleep that night, having lost so much of her joy and pleasure on account of that man she desires and loves. Between her teeth she often bemoans the fact that she does not know what she should say. She often gives a start, heaves frequent sighs, and repeatedly calls to the knight: 'Oh Fergus, my dear handsome love! – My love? Fool that I am, what have I said? He never saw me except today, never at all before this very day. And do I then have the nerve to dare call him "my love"? Now people can say and prove that I'm both foolish and base to want to trouble myself over that man whom I never saw before in my life, and who hasn't yet spoken to me. And very early tomorrow he'll leave on his way; and once he has gone off tomorrow he'll not remember me. I don't know why he should remember; for it's neither possible nor right for him to acquire a sweetheart wherever he takes lodging. Now he's to leave at daybreak tomorrow.

1826   'What? Will it then be this love that will kill me in such a fashion? He will be guilty of murdering me if he slays me in this brutal way. Alas! If he only knew how I love him faithfully from my heart, he would never behave so wickedly as not to have mercy on me. He never will know unless I tell him. – Tell him? Now I've said something foolish with which I'll bring shame on my family: I'd rather be put in my coffin than make the first amorous approaches to him. – What shall I do, then? I'll flee! I shall come to forget this love and don't care to hear any more about it. My father wants to marry me to a king, a powerful man and perhaps a more handsome one than this. – More handsome? Now I've spoken nonsense: there's certainly no more handsome or well-made man than he this side of Pavia. If he knew here and now how I've slandered him, I'm sure he would definitely not love me. – Love? He doesn't love me in the least. He shows me no sign of it. If he had any sort of love for me, I imagine that last evening he would have asked me, with a show of love and tenderness, to become his sweetheart. But perhaps he didn't know how to.

1858   'What business, then, do I have with either him or his affections? Should I lust after his great physical beauty? Tomorrow when he leaves here his beauty won't stay behind, but will keep him company. And what has that to do with me? Perhaps I'd like to

rob him of his beauty and his courage? That I'll never do, by
Saint Vincent! I've no wish for that: on the contrary, I would
increase them, if it were in my power to do so!'

1871   Such is the maiden's suffering. First she sobs, then she yawns;
she tosses and turns, then gives a start and almost loses conscious-
ness. At one moment she says something, at the next denies it,
now weeping, now laughing. Then she turns her bed upside
down, so violent are the joustings of love. These are the payments
and rewards Love gives to the knights he keeps in his private
company. He has given the maiden full payment, having made
her fall in love with, in my opinion, the very noblest young knight
in all the world. It is, though, her misfortune to be the only one
wounded and suffering the anguish of it; and in that he has made
it so much worse for her.

1890   *In the end she decided to get up from her bed, however
hard she found it, and go to the knight, who was fast asleep
without any thought for her; nor did he know what love is,
never having experienced its pain. Galiene jumps up in great
agitation and her hair in disorder, taking nothing but her shift,
over which she threw a mantle lined with grey fur. At once she
tiptoed softly to the bedroom door, not wanting anyone to
hear her and afraid of being spotted. She went up to the bed
where Fergus lay asleep and pondered for a long while on how
she should address him. She very nearly goes back to bed in
her own room. Love told her to make a direct approach to the
knight; but shame forbids her ever to be so brazen as to tell
Fergus what she has in mind. Renewing his assault on her, Love
told her there was nothing for it but to confess to the knight,
because he will never be so miserly with his heart as not to
have pity on her if she appeals to him.

1922   Kneeling down before him, she very fearfully raises the coverlet and sheets, feeling as she does a great love for him. Weeping
hot tears, she places her hand on his breast. He wakes in great
alarm to see her on her knees and with her face wet with the
warm tears she had shed. He drew her a little towards him and

said to her: 'Now I've got you! Tell me what you've come here for, and be sure not to hide anything from me!' The maiden replies very meekly: 'My friend, good sir, I've submitted to great torture on your account, for I could not be more in love with you. I've lost my heart unless I can find someone to tell me what's happened to it, for it's come here to you. Please give it back to me!'

1944   Fergus replies: 'Your heart, young lady? I've never seen it. I wouldn't give it up on any account if I did have it in my possession; but you may be sure I have no part of it.' – 'Ah, sir knight, don't say that! It really is entirely yours. Why have you not noticed, when it's totally at your service – and I am too, if you wish? Your handsome body, your beauty, your valour and prowess have put me in a state of such dire distress that I shall never find joy or gladness unless it be through you. Have no doubt that you hold in your hand both my death and my life.'

1961   With a laugh Fergus replies: 'Maiden, my quest is for something other than love and its pleasures. First I want to settle a fight I'm pledged to. But on my return, if I get out of it alive, I'll come back this way. Then, if you wish, you shall freely have my love and affection. But give me time enough to speak with that knight who is so fiercely arrogant. For, as God is my witness, there's nothing that could induce me to give a maiden my affection or love her before I've vanquished, overcome in armed combat or killed or captured that knavish knight.'

1982   The maiden sees at once that he will do nothing for her. In a swoon she falls back on the stone floor. Then, when she comes to, she disparages Love and all his power, swearing that, on the contrary, he is totally blind* to have so wounded her on account of that man in whom she has found no pity, affection or tenderness. Full of grief and consternation she jumps up like a mad woman. Going into her room, she throws herself on her bed. Scorning all joy, she now hates herself and longs for death. She knows nothing that might bring her comfort, but wonders what to do. At one moment she said she would kill herself and put an end to her grief. At another she said she would not, for that would be a quite outrageous act: never once had any woman of her family killed herself for love. After that she said that in the morning at first light she would slip out of the court without leave or her uncle's knowledge; and she would go to Lothian, for it was already a year since she had been with her father. Now she will go and carry out his wishes in order to take her mind off her love. She was really confident of being able to snuff out that love burning within her and inflaming her, to her great anguish.* She remains preoccupied with these thoughts until the dawn appears and day breaks.

2019   Fergus rose early and asked for his equipment. It is brought without demur, and he proceeds to put it on. Once armed to his satisfaction, he mounted the charger they had made ready for him, after which he asked his leave of his host and the girl. She kept her face bowed low and found it hard to utter a word to him. Putting spurs to the horse, Fergus rides out through the castle gate. The horse dashes off with him; and his host escorts him until he has shown him the direct cross-country road leading to the Black Mountain. But he begs him before they part that, if the combat ends to his honour and advantage, he return by way of his home. Fergus gives him his firm assurance that, provided no other adventure detains him, once he has the horn and wimple he will return by the castle.

2045   With that he parts from his host. He comes riding along the edge of a mighty forest, asking frequently and making enquiries of the passers-by he sees about the road he can take to go and fight the wicked knight, for whom he has no love or affection. He finds many people to direct him. Fergus comes onto a very wide plain between two hills. On he rode past hillocks and deep valleys until he saw a mountain appear that reached up to the clouds and supported the entire sky. In the world there is no living animal however nimble or powerful which could climb up this mountain unless it had wings to fly, except that on one side there was a wild track constructed by a giant who lived in the

forest. But no horse can tackle it: the man wishing to climb it
will have to go on foot or else stay at the bottom of the mountain, because the track is so narrow, straight up the mountain,
that no one would ever climb up by it unless he were more agile
than other men.

2077   Fergus looks upwards and easily recognises the mountain he
has sought and enquired about for so long. He is delighted to
have found it, but is dismayed by one thing, namely that he sees
clearly that he has to climb this mountain on foot. He does not
know where to put his steed, because he expects to lose it if he
leaves it behind. Then he hurries to the forest and finds a very
tall olive tree* fairer than any on earth. All the other knights in
quest of this adventure used to hitch their horses to it when
they arrived. There Fergus tethers his own strong, fine mount;
and, removing the shield from his neck, he hangs that on the
olive tree, against which he props his great lance. Then he
swiftly climbs up the mountain, his drawn sword giving him the
appearance of a man fully on the alert against being surprised
by the knight. He is more afraid the man may take his horse
than he is of fighting him. He struggles hard up the mountain,
laden as he is with his arms; and often he missed his footing,
but clung onto the small branches and the briars that grew by
them along the track. Such was his suffering, his determination,
toil and tribulation as he clambered up the Nouquetran. When
he reached the top, you cannot wonder that he was somewhat
exhausted. Not a limb of his did not ache then, no finger or toe,
however small.

2117   He paused a little and looked around him to see the great,
wide forest as far as the Irish Sea. He can see England and
Cornwall.* But now he is firmly convinced that the information
he was given is false in that he has not at once found the lion in
the middle of the path. But for some time before it is seen he will
have sought and hunted for it on foot over the mountain-top;
*for it was in a most handsome, beautiful chapel, in which there
was no scrap of timber: it was rather entirely of marble and

decorated with carvings. The doors were of ivory and the door-way gilded.

2136   In front, at the entrance, was an amazing great churl: you never saw one so hideous. He was cast in bronze, and in his hand, to be sure, he held a huge, heavy steel hammer. If you had seen the churl, you would not have said otherwise than that he looked like a mortal man; and you would certainly have expected him to strike you with the hammer, had you wanted to go inside. But he could move neither sideways nor forwards nor back any more than a stone could have done. That churl had been made so impressive that there was not this side of Constantinople any man so bold or proud that, should he come close to him, he would have failed to be terrified – and pointlessly, because it would have been possible to go right up to him in safety. But that is how the man who guarded the lion had had him constructed, and in that way he frightened everybody.

2161   Night and day the lion rests in that chapel. However, it quite lacks flesh and blood, skin and hair: instead, it is completely white, beautifully carved in ivory. Round its neck by a silver chain has been hung the horn, and with it the wimple. Fergus goes seeking the entrance, having found the chapel; and he sees the churl standing guarding the door and entrance. Then he has the idea of going to ask the churl about the lion, should he know of it. Going straight up to the churl, he said: 'Don't keep me in the dark, fellow: where can I find the lion I'm searching for over this mountain?' The other does not reply a single word, being incapable of doing so. Fergus is quite amazed at that, thinking he ought to speak. He will again attempt to ask him whereabouts he might find it, the lion, if he knew; so once more he asks him. 'Fellow,' says he, 'by the faith you owe me, give me directions for finding the lion I've been looking for for so long.' The other did not utter a word.

2192   Fergus almost went out of his mind with anger and annoyance, really thinking that the churl was doing this out of contempt. Fergus raises to his shoulder a rock which lay there;

for he wants to do that stupid churl a real injury, if he can. But he dares not go close to him on account of the great hammer in his grasp, not himself having a shield or buckler for protection, should he make to strike him with the hammer. That made him fearful. Nevertheless he hurled the heavy rock he was holding so that it struck him hard on the chest and broke both his arms. The hammer promptly fell from his grasp. Seeing the hammer on the ground, Fergus proceeds to attack him with his sword, striking two-handed for all he is worth. And the churl does not budge. Then he is ashamed and sorry to have struck so violently something that cannot move. He would not at any price want that to become known at the royal court: it would be a great scandal. They will never get to hear of it, if he can help it.

2222   Thereupon he enters the chapel, looks in front of him and sees the horn and the wimple hanging there round the lion's neck. If anyone should give him without stint all the gold there is beneath the firmament, he would have felt no more joy in his heart than he derived from this adventure. He goes with all speed to the lion and promptly takes from it the horn and wimple too. Then he hurries outside, since there was nothing else he was seeking.

2235   Fergus sets the horn to his lips. Three times he sounds it with all his might, so that its call has carried over the entire countryside.* The horn's voice could be heard for four full leagues in all directions, provoking a hubbub of shouting throughout the district, with everybody quick to say: 'Who now is that unhappy wretch so anxious to die? He certainly didn't have much regard for his life when he climbed the mountain to sound the horn. It would have been far better for him to steal that horn, if he wanted it. That wasn't a very good idea of his, make no mistake about it! Had he known the grim game shortly to be arranged for him, he would never have headed that way.' That was what the people were saying. They all voiced grave misgivings regarding Fergus without wishing him any harm, but full of grief and fear lest the Black Knight, wicked brigand that he was, should treacherously slay him. He, Fergus, has no fears in that respect, but expects to return to court without any trouble.

2265   He proceeds to descend the mountain with the horn hanging from his neck and holding the wimple in his hand. He comes as quickly as possible to his horse, which had been left under the olive tree. He was delighted when he found it; and he mounted it with great vigour, then took up his lance and shield. If he should now find two knights, or three or four spoiling for a fight, he would never hold himself back. Then, after waiting there only a short while, he heard a loud drumming of hoofbeats galloping through the forest in his direction, making a din and clamour as if all the rutting stags in the forest were gathering there: they would have made no greater noise. Fergus stayed briefly under the olive tree, supposing that some knights had come there into the forest to hunt the stag, boar, roebuck or doe. If he has his way, he will never leave before he knows the truth.

2290   Leaning on his saddle-bow, he looks ahead along the gravelled track and sees the knight approaching more swiftly than a lightning-strike. There was nothing white about him except his teeth; his horse and armour were black. But he does not in the least reassure the man he sees beneath the olive tree. He begins to bawl loudly at him in furious indignation: 'Hey, who are you, you miserable wretch holding that wimple and horn? You know quite well they're mine! Are you one of the knights of that very wicked, abject King Arthur? His arrogance has been truly deflated. He's not worthy to be a king, because he daren't even put his trust in his own courage to enter this land in quest of the horn and wimple. Instead he sends his menials who have come from other countries to serve at court as hirelings, when he's not prepared to take them permanently into his company. What's the reason for Gawain, Lancelot, Erec and Yvain not coming? Or Sagremor the Impetuous, or that ninny Perceval? Or else let that disreputable, cowardly king bring with him twenty knights, or his whole army should he want to. He's very craven to be so afraid of me. But this much honour I'll do him: before midday comes I'll send him your head by the lowest of my serving-lads, just to bring him shame and vexation. It's unlucky for you that you entered his service!'

2329   Fergus hears the man threatening him. He braces himself and sets the shield on his arm, for he is remarkably upset by his speaking so disgracefully to him about both the king and his nobles. Now he does not consider himself worth two buttons unless he can avenge the king. He braces himself on the charger, puts his lance in the rest and then lowers it, and charges at the Black Knight without offering any challenge or reply. Each of them gives his horse free rein and lets it have its head. With their lances they deal each other mighty blows, putting into them all their strength. Fergus strikes the knight as hard as he can with his keen, sharp spear, piercing his shield and rending his hauberk. The steel grazes his side, but does him no damage or injury. And the knight strikes him in turn, attacking him so savagely that he pierced his shield and holed his hauberk, ripping out the links. The lance passed a yard and more behind him, but without touching his flesh at all.

2356   The Black Knight taunts Fergus, as you shall hear: 'Fellow, there's no way for you to stand up to my blows. I fancy your hauberk's well holed at the back, because by my reckoning my spear went more than six feet through it. It was very considerate of the tip not to bother doing you any harm!' When Fergus hears him, he is most mortified and almost goes out of his mind with rage. He flung his retort at the knight: 'Do you think you'll win with insults? What can you want from me? If you've pierced my shield, what have you gained so far by that? It seems to me you've felt just now the cold of my steel rubbing against your side. Only the Devil stopped it running you through the body!'

2378   With that, each of them retrieves his lance, and they charge at each other. Holding their lances outstretched, they clash together on equal terms. Both these fine knights are full of valour, for neither makes the other give ground. It appears that the Black Knight did suffer a slight misfortune; for Fergus has shattered and holed both his shield and his hauberk, having thrust his lance-tip into his body so that it came out on the other side, and the lance broke into pieces. But the knight was not a whit dismayed by any harm he had suffered, giving no sign from his appearance or demeanour that he felt any discomfort or pain. He proceeds to strike Fergus full on his shield with its floral painting; and his lance split and shivered right to his fist. Seeing this, Fergus offers him a greeting: 'God save you, sir knight! Now you're in need of a bleeding, as is very clear to me from the sight of your blood on that shining hauberk. It's flowing too freely: do at least be careful! For the blood-letter's a novice and didn't know how to pick the right vein. I'm afraid you may have some trouble and pain from this blood-letting: I think a vein's been severed, and you really need to have it staunched. I've sent my spear fishing in your belly below your breast. Your prattling and villainous crime were unlucky for you, because today they'll cost you your life!'

2417   The knight does not think all of Fergus' talk worth a glove. He was more arrogant, bold and offensive than ever, and actually drew his sword at once. He holds his stout shield on his arm, then sets spurs to his charger and goes to deal with Fergus, who draws his own sword in turn. This signals the start of a hard, bitter combat between them, greater than was ever before fought between two armed men in so short a time. They launch themselves at each other like lions, raining blows with their sharp swords that make their helmets ring and sparks fly from them. Their shields lie in splinters on the meadow around them. Never in their whole lives would the two of them have called off the combat: instead, both of them would have come to grief had it not finally been for a serious accident suffered by the knight. For at one pass he made, he broke his steel sword in two. When he saw his sword snap, he was filled with rage: he thinks about it, but does not know what to do. Now he would have wished to be back at home! It is useless for him to retreat: if he can get out of this alive, he will have to surrender, for there is no point in fleeing.

2451   When he sees there is no alternative, he dismounts from his good steed and clasps his two hands together. His heart palpitates with terror. Then he kneels in obeisance and begs Fergus for mercy. Hearing him call for mercy, Fergus thinks to himself: 'If I kill him, this knight I've beaten, I'll get little praise for that. If he dies, it's a great pity for he's brave and valiant but for his insolent conduct. It's much better that I should send him to the king who made me a knight and that he should give himself up to him as his prisoner and take with him the wimple and horn on my behalf. If he does this, I ask nothing more of him.' He at once bends down and, taking him by his round helmet, says: 'Get up straight away, sir knight! I'll forget my grudge against you if you do me a service according to my wishes and conditions. It is to go and surrender to the king and take with you this horn and this wimple; and you must place yourself entirely at his mercy, however unhappy you may feel about it. That's my wish and my pleasure. Otherwise you'll die by my sword, unless you say you will go.'

2485   – 'Ah, mercy, sir knight! I don't know that any of my friends are where you want to send me. I'll on no account go to that place or region, for fear of my life. The king hates me from the bottom of his heart. If he held me in captivity, all the gold on earth wouldn't get me out without his having me torn limb from limb. I'd rather die than go there, for I've done him much wrong. I've slain many a knight of his with my great sword that is now shattered. Kill me, if you wish, because he'd kill me just the same.' – 'Good sir knight,' he replies, 'you've no need at all to fear that: you can go there in confidence. I think I'm well enough in with the king: so that he'll do you no harm, tell him I'm sending you to him. I'm certain he will pardon you and forget all his anger and resentment. What's more, a hundred silver marks is the cost of a single day's delay: go there now, and don't argue! Greet the king for me, and all the others except Kay, who made fun of me at court. He'll certainly pay for that if I can find the opportunity, whoever it may please or annoy!'

2517   Once he has heard Fergus priding himself like this on being so
        well favoured at court, the Black Knight will go there, come what
        may, like a man anxious to stay alive if he can. He says to him:
        'Good sir, I'll go to court. I'll mention your name and will, if you
        wish, take that wimple you're holding and also that horn to good
        King Arthur; and I'll throw myself on his mercy as a defeated
        man, never fear.' He then swears and pledges him that he will
        take the wimple to the king and place himself at his mercy,
        fully armed as he is here. Having accepted his pledge to his satis-
        faction and liking, Fergus proceeded at once to hand over to him
        the horn and silk wimple. With that they take to the road and
        part company on the understanding that the knight will go
        straight to the court once he is fit again, that his message will be
        delivered to all the lords and to the king, and he will also tell my
        lord Kay everything he wishes him to say.

2546   Fergus goes off across a heath, riding at great speed and asking
        about adventures, but unable to find any. Then he declared his
        intention to return by way of his host, who had begged him to do
        so when he took his leave of him. He will not deny him his wish.
        In the evening he arrived at Liddel to find his host relaxing on the
        bridge as he had been the previous evening. But in the hall old
        and young, tall and short are in the throes of great grief. The
        lord, however, was there on the bridge deep in thought; for to his
        profound sorrow he had lost his niece. He did not know what
        had become of her, and this filled his heart with sadness and
        dejection. Fergus hastened to where he saw his host. From his
        features he could clearly tell that he was not full of gaiety.
        Greeting him in the name of God the Father, he asks him to tell
        him truly the cause of his heavy heart.

2573   Without hesitation the host replied: 'Sir, it's no wonder that
        I'm despondent: this very day I've lost all my joy and affection,
        my gladness and delight – my niece, that is, whom I loved so
        much. While I was escorting you, she slipped out of my court, I
        don't know why, without ever taking leave of me; and I know no
        reason at all for this. So I'm extremely afraid for her, leaving as

she did completely on her own for some district unknown to me. I've no idea where to go to look for her, whether in Ireland, England, Scotland* or Lothian. Ah, I believed that in no corner of the world could a maiden be found who was her equal in courtliness and intelligence. I'm very puzzled by this journey and the way in which she gave me the slip, never having spoken to us about it. But now we must drop the subject: the time has come to go to our quarters as evening is here. Let's go! You're exhausted and, I think, suffering from bearing your arms. It's time to take lodging for the night. Your hauberk's full of holes: you've had an encounter with some knights – that's obvious from your shield. How did you fare? Don't keep anything from me, in God's name!'

2608 Fergus, whose thoughts were so set on his sweetheart that he had become disorientated, said: 'Sir, in God's name, tell me truly if the bright-faced maiden has left these parts without your knowing where or in what direction.' – 'Yes, sir, so help me God! She really has gone off, and I'm very depressed about it. But tell me your news.' Fergus replied: 'Come now, sir host, as God's your help, haven't you offended the courtly damsel in any way? Upon my soul, I'm terribly upset that she has gone off like this!' They stayed there together quite as long as it takes to walk a league, talking of this and that, quite forgetting about the lodging, the host speaking of one thing, he replying at cross-purposes. One of them asks about the combat, the other is in the toils and tribulations of love. The host enquires about the Black Knight, and Fergus fails to obtain information about the maiden he has lost.

2634 *Love accuses him, Love blames him, Love burns him with his spark. His heart and desire are continuously directed towards the maiden. Love, I think, has vanquished and overcome in a very short time that man whose conquest no lady had ever as yet in any way achieved. Now Love is his lord and master and keeps making him pay for the fact that he dared to refuse the maiden who sought his affection and committed herself entirely to him without sharing her favours with any other. Now he repents, but

too late: too late he has found repentance. He will have to suffer
many a hardship and endure many adventures before he can find
her again, for he does not know to what region the maiden has
gone. Had he known, he would search for her and not hold back
for fear of any adventure or enchantment. What had happened
to her depresses him, robbing him of joy and pleasure; and he
does not know if it is day or night, evening or morning.

2662   Seeing him so dispirited and dejected, his host enquired of
him why he was brooding so. He replies: 'I have good cause for
thought, and should despise myself more than any other living
man. If I'm ashamed, it's only right I should be: no one at all
should feel sorry for me on that account. I only wish my grief
were greater. The rustic has said straight out: "Someone who
flings underfoot what he can hold in his hands should not be
allowed to continue dwelling among other people." It's been
disastrous for me that what I was so sure of I've become a laugh-
ing-stock by losing. I'll just never get it back again! I've heard the
saying that a man with everything he wants may try to get something that brings him grief. Alas! It's really my own fault that I've
brought this grief on myself. – My fault? More my misfortune.
Rather, indeed, it's in my nature only to act shamefully. Who am
I, then? – What's that to me? I'm stupid to dabble in love. My
father Soumillet never in all his living days indulged in that sort
of thing, yet his son wants to do so! God! How ridiculous I am to
want to join the ranks of those who night and day serve as Love's
mercenaries! – And why should I not join them? For then I'd
increase my worth. Why not? Because it seems to me I ought
indeed to have a beautiful mistress.

2701   '– A mistress? Where is there to be found one more attractive
and charming than she whom I've recklessly lost? It's a wonder I
don't go mad with rage: that would be only just, when I rebuffed
the one who paid court to me. It should turn out to my great
shame. Alas! If I thought now I could find her in any land, I'd go
in search of her and never give up at all until I'd found her. No,
there's no route so perilous this side of the Dead Sea that I

wouldn't gladly take it to seek the most excellent lady in the world. Nevertheless, may God confound me if I ever once give up! And I shall find no joy or happiness and never again be free from suffering until I've heard definite news of her somewhere or other. Nor shall I ever again so long as I live hear tell of an adventure which I'll not undertake to prove myself in valour and prowess. I'll never shirk it out of laziness or fear of meeting my end; for I'd be glad to have found in some country a knight to vanquish me in arms or slice my head from my body, because then my suffering would be over!'

2733   Thus Fergus laments. This resolve of his grew, bringing such hardships and adventures as will prove trying, difficult and protracted for him. He will have many troubles and adversities before he hears any news of her. His joy turns to sadness. He has lost very nearly all of the great prowess and valour he showed the previous morning. Love torments and harasses him, reminding him of the beauty he had seen in his sweetheart and of her courtliness and intelligence. He does not know if the weather is wet or fair or whether it is evening or morning. He held his head bowed for a long time beneath his helmet. His host, a very courtly man, clearly noticed this. He loses no time, but takes him at once by the skirt of his hauberk, saying: 'Sir, if you please, there's no need for you to grieve like this: it's not right for you to be distressed. It's not fitting for a knight like you ever to make such a show on account of a maid or a woman, lest you be thought childish. You should leave off! The distress is my affair, and it's up to me to do the grieving. But this is not your concern, so let it be: there's no need for it! Let's go and take our lodging for the night. I'll entertain you very well; and on your account I shall pull myself out of the grief that's so tormenting me because of my niece whom I've lost and never expect to see again.'

2774   Fergus heard what his host said about entertaining him very well and that he would cheer himself up completely out of his own depression and great grief in order to honour him and make him happy. But that is in no way possible, since he well knows

that he would not find the graceful, exquisite person of the
maiden as he had the previous evening. For that reason he was
less than keen to stay, but said: 'My good host, that's impossible.
My sadness forbids me to take a lodging from now on for the rest
of my days. I'll not take shelter for my comfort in any hamlet,
town or castle until I get to know in what country the maiden,
your niece, is to be found: of that you may be certain. So your
offers to me of shelter and a lodging will be in vain. All the
people from here to the sea would be unable to induce me to take
a lodging on my journey while I'm in my present state of grief
and troubled thoughts. Give me my leave: I'm going!' His host
sees plainly that it is not for him to choose to keep the young
gentleman back: like it or not, he gives his leave. And Fergus does
not linger with him, but sets off with his shield at his neck and
his lance in his grasp.

2806   *Before he had gone very far, the sun began to set, and evening
fell quickly. Fergus rode through a dense forest that evening; but
it was a great advantage to him that the moon was shining very
brightly, since that night, it seems, it was full. I believe it was past
midnight when Fergus, with raised lance, brooding and dejected,
entered a glade: it was small, by no means large, but more attractive than any other in the forest. In the middle of it was a tent in
which a bold, doughty, proud knight was lying. He had never
found his match, able to overcome him in armed combat; and he
was the lord of the glade. Fergus sees him and reins his good
steed in that direction to find, in front of the tent, a porter, who
was ugly and misshapen and only three feet tall. He had a huge
head and flat brow, a snub nose like a cat's and great wide
nostrils. His lips looked like two steaks. He was shaggy, black-
haired, and humped like a camel. In his hand he held a stick.

2838   When he first saw Fergus approaching, he shouted to him:
'Steady now, sir knight! You could well be in too much of a hurry.
It would be better for you to turn back than come here, make no
mistake! If my lord were awake now, you'd have a very costly
tribute to pay: you'd leave your head behind as a pledge!' Hearing

the porter's call, Fergus immediately comes out of his reverie and makes straight for the pavilion. The rogue raises his stick and brings it down between the horse's ears, knocking away virtually all the flesh around its right eye. You may be certain that Fergus was extremely upset to see the rascal strike his steed in this way. He will now avenge it or die in the attempt. He drives his gold-plated spurs hard into the horse, takes the scoundrel by the hair and so strikes and thumps him and has him trampled by the horse that he very nearly kills him. As it is, with the blood spurting from his ears, he roars and shouts at the top of his voice.

2866   Then the knight, startled by the great din, wakes and is quite astonished: 'Who's this who is so bold as to attack my tent and make my dwarf yell so much?' He did not choose to arm himself, but pulled on a pair of breeches and a shirt and quickly threw a tunic of Friesland cloth* onto his back. Taking a large steel sword in his hand, he came at top speed to where the dwarf was bawling his head off, with the intention of rescuing him. When he noticed the arms with which Fergus was accoutred, you may be sure he was much alarmed and in fear of his life. There is no man this side of Namur, I imagine, however bold he might be, who would not have been in mortal terror in his situation. Nevertheless, he gave no sign of being in the least afraid of this knight he sees fully armed.

2890   He goes striding up to him and starts shouting in a loud voice: 'Let my dwarf go, fellow! Take your hands off him! You're acting basely, beating him before my very eyes. By Him who created the beasts, if I were armed as you are, you'd really pay dearly for having so battered and beaten that dwarf!' Fergus answers the knight: 'There's a magistrate in this district: you'd do well to lay a complaint with him, if I've done you any wrong. Alternatively, if I don't make you satisfactory amends, then don't hesitate to dispossess me of such lands as I hold from you until I've made you reparation for my offence in respect of your hunchback dwarf. And if you're not satisfied with this proposal, go away and arm yourself, if you have your equipment with you; and I'll

wait for you out here until you've dressed yourself up nicely and
handsomely in your gear. After that, if it suits you and you want
to fight with me, then shame on me if I don't agree!'*

2919   In the tent was an attractive maiden, courtly and beautiful,
who was the knight's mistress. She was wakened by the noise and
jumped up, with her hair all dishevelled like a mad woman. Out
of the pavilion she went, wearing nothing but a mantle of fine
material, which she had wrapped tightly round her. She looks
across and sees her lover approaching with the bleeding dwarf.
He shouts sharply to her: 'Go back again, maiden, and bring me
my equipment because, by the faith I owe you, I'm about to have
to fight a foolhardy knight who has all but killed my dwarf. I'll
not care to go on living unless I can quickly lay him low!' When
the maiden hears that, she dashes back at once and gives him his
arms. He promptly puts them on, donning his favourite hauberk
and lacing on his steel helmet. He girds the sword on his left side.
The maiden brought him a good white horse of his, which he
mounted at once, the maiden holding his stirrup for him: he had
no other squire at all. Then, hanging his shield at his neck and
taking a keen, stout lance, he rode out of the tent with a clatter.

2954   Fiercely and angrily he yells just like a demon. 'Now, fellow,'
he says, 'on your guard! I'm challenging you: you may be certain
of that. The dwarf you've unjustly beaten will be grimly avenged.'
Grasping his shield, he brandished the lance and at once set
spurs to the horse. Fergus does the same to his own by no means
sluggish mount, pricking it with his silver spurs. Each goads his
own steed hard and lets it have free rein. The horses have big
hearts, and the noble knights get the most out of them. They
clash impetuously together so that each knocks the other backwards, and the challenger is quite unbalanced. With the tip of his
keen, sharp lance Fergus gives him a mighty blow high on the
shield to knock it down against his chest. He loses both his stirrups. Fergus thrusts hard, and he falls.

2978   Seeing him on the ground, Fergus hurls these words at him:
'Sir knight, you were naïve to boast prematurely that your dwarf

would be avenged once you had your gear. It seems to me rather
that things are worse now than before, because your shame is all
the greater now I see you doing somersaults in the meadow here.
What I've heard said is true: that a man may think to avenge his
shame, but instead increases and deepens it. That's just what
you've done. But a hundred curses on anyone who is sorry for
you! Get up quickly – you're too slow! If your backside had teeth,
I fancy it would have given you a nasty nip. By a hundred living
devils! In what country did you learn to ride? Woe betide the
man who had the job of teaching you arms and horsemanship!'
Hearing this provocation, the knight showed his boldness by
jumping up, drawing his polished sword from its sheath. Then he
made for the charger he saw straying about there and promptly
mounted it, since Fergus did not prevent him from doing so, but
waited quite peacefully until he was back in the saddle.

3009   Then they return to the fray, each grasping his polished, sharp-
pointed sword. Now the combat begins again; and with the noise
of their clashing arms they make the leafy woodland resound.
Each repays the other all he owes, in full and on time. They were
both gallant knights: bold, valiant and good fighters, and strong
and dashing as well. But Fergus delivered a not ineffective stroke
with his sword, dealing his companion with all his might a well-
placed blow on the green helmet that shone as if it were crystal.
He knocks off the entire back half. Now the knight will need to
look for a doctor! For the steel sword is keen, and it shaves away
the hair and skin at the back of the skull and slices off a portion
of his shield. Had the blow not been deflected, it would have
cloven him down to the feet.

3035   Fergus sees this and rails at him: 'Knight, just look at your
sweetheart! Ride on for love of her! See what a fresh complexion
she has: that should really cheer you up! – But I see you're bleeding here. By the faith I owe that bright moon, now you look like
Fortune, who has hair on the front of her head, but is bald at the
back.* I'd always understood that people were hairless on the
face side: but you're bald behind!' – 'That's the present fashion!'

says the knight in turn. 'A curse on the edges of your sword that it cuts so well! Never before have I known such a hard or deadly fight.' Fergus replies: 'And you won't anywhere else. That's what happens in this game: when two brave, valiant men fight together without giving ground, one or other comes to grief. But that's not yet happened in your case: you're too proud and courageous – and quite right too, for no one should show cowardice in front of his sweetheart.'

3063   The knight sweats with rage; but he has already lost his strength through the blood draining from his wound. He does not know what to do and is in great dismay. Had he thought he would find Fergus merciful, he would go and appeal to him. Nevertheless, he will try him to see if he can obtain mercy from him. He steps forward. 'Mercy!' he calls to him, handing over his polished sword and begging him to spare his life. He will always be his man alone, to serve him as his lord, since he has overcome him by force. Fergus took the fine sword, after which he stipulated that, if he wishes to win his affection and escape from there with his life, he should go and give himself up to King Arthur immediately, without any delay, and should take with him his lovely sweetheart. The knight fully consents and pledges that he will go just as soon as day comes, and the dwarf and his sweetheart with him. With that the contest is at an end. Fergus leaves, and the knight remains, turning pale and wan with pain.

3091   The night passes, and the day arrives. Fergus pursues his journey quite alone, and immerses himself in his thoughts. He did not, though, forget his lance, with which he had felled the knight. He rode through the forest that day until about noon without drinking or eating or thinking about food. He holds his head bowed under his helmet. Again and again he laments for his love; and he lets his horse go wherever it wishes, its reins slack, until he comes to a causeway beside a turbulent, fast-flowing river. Many a noble man had met his end there. On the causeway was a tower built by a robber. He always lurked in that lair, never wearying of doing evil, in order to rob passers-by;

and, when they put up no resistance, he killed them on the spot. He had lived there for a long time, committing many crimes in the district until its reputation was such that no one dared go there any more. Now, whatever his wishes, Fergus will have to pass that way; but he knew nothing of the robber lying in wait in his ambush.

3122   He goes riding along until he sees a round fortress and below it a great bridge, by which one crossed the moats. Fergus arrives there deep in thought assuming he would be able to pass over freely without waiting: but things will not go as he expects. For that man who had concentrated all his attention, mind and thought on doing evil comes galloping out of the fortress shouting at the top of his voice: 'Be more sensible, sir knight! You pay tribute here when you want to travel in this region. You think you'll cheat me out of it, but it will turn out quite differently. By Him who created the firmament, the sun and the moon, I'll teach you the custom before you leave me! Get down off that horse, because it's mine as my tribute!' On hearing him Fergus replied: 'Sir vassal, are you challenging me for my horse and telling me you've a right to it? Damn anyone who had that idea and brought it here for you! By my soul, one of us will pay for it first, either you or I!'

3154   With that they both charge angrily at each other. Fergus strikes the knight first, and with such remarkable force that he snapped the arm with which he held his shield clean across. The robber feels himself wounded and sees his arm broken and crippled. Then, as he had had no experience of such blows and it seems to him totally evident that, should his opponent find the opportunity to deal him an equally heavy stroke, he will have him vanquished and slain, he has no care to receive another. He takes flight, lance in rest, heading for his lair as hard as he can go. Fergus, in pursuit, is concerned to get him before he reaches the fortress. He drives his spurs into Arondiel,* who carries him faster than the wind; and he shouts at the top of his voice: 'Come back here, sir knight! I'm bringing you my charger because you want to be paid the toll you're demanding. I wouldn't on any account want you to think me a trickster or a base, very obstinate fellow by taking away your crossing fee. Wait for me, and I'll give it to you and then be on my way, for I've still a long journey ahead of me.'

3186   The other, however, has no wish to stop or receive the toll. He would rather be back home well shut in his tower than out there with Fergus. But that is not to be: he will not get inside and will be more miserable and vexed than ever before. Fergus gives hot pursuit and follows and chases him until the horse on which the robber was mounted caught one of its hooves and tripped, falling into a mire. The other, in his headlong pursuit, dashed past before wheeling and coming back. He found the robber lying on his shield face upwards, miserable and dejected in the mire. Fergus looks at him and shouts: 'Would you be needing help, sir knight? As God may watch over you, I'd be very glad to help you, if I were sure of being let off the toll I owe you.' The robber said: 'Have pity on me, noble knight, by God almighty! I'll be your vassal from now on and will serve you to the best of my ability all my living days.'

3217   Fergus replies: 'Enough of that! You'll die straight away by my steel sword, unless you assure and pledge me that you will never again haunt this region to rob or harass honest people. Instead, you'll go on my behalf to give yourself up at the court of King Arthur, who the other day dubbed me knight and gave me this equipment. If you're prepared to do that promptly, I think you may survive.' The robber gives him his word and pledges that he will do that directly, and will go straight to Carlisle. Fergus replies: 'Then there's nothing more I wish to ask or demand.' With that he heads back, and the other goes up to the castle. Fergus crosses the bridge, which nobody had ever crossed since the robber he had vanquished had first frequented the place. Now he has paid the toll; and henceforth people can come and go there safely and without fear.

3243   *Fergus goes thinking of his beloved until he is so plagued and tortured by hunger that he does not know what to do. If he now had bushels of silver, he would freely give it all up to have his fill of bread; and it is no wonder he felt like eating, because he had not tasted bread or clear spring-water for two whole days. Now he has fallen into a serious plight. Now his hunger makes him forget the great weight on his mind concerning his dear sweetheart. Ahead he caught sight of a hazy cloud and saw a great deal of smoke rising on a slope beside a rock. Then he draws the firm conclusion that charcoal-burners have come to work in the forest. Whipping and spurring his good steed to a fast gallop, he does not pause until he draws near to the rock and sees there a very prettily constructed bower. Inside it was a huge fire, and seated round the fire he saw fifteen knights who were not old or grey-haired, but all youthful. They lived continually by plundering, night and day, in the forest: that was their only livelihood. They had come from winning some booty and had sat down to a meal just at the time we call noon.

3280   On seeing this, Fergus drops the reins of his northern horse and comes straight to the rock where he has seen these men making merry. He has every intention of sharing their meal, whoever may pull a long face or grumble: he is very much in need of it. Necessity is the cause of many misdeeds: they say that need knows no law. Fergus dismounts from his charger and puts down the strong shield slung at his neck and the ashen lance. He does not greet or address any of them. Leaving his horse where it is, he unlaces his helmet as quickly as possible and goes straight to the bower. The very gallant Fergus took a loaf of wheaten bread that was in front of the chief of the knights: it was large and uncut. There were capons turning over a fire, and he seized the spit with both hands – how he managed to do it I do not know. Without any fuss or bother, he removed one of the capons and ate heartily from it. From under their noses he took a cup full to the brim with spiced wine and drank it at a single draught.

3310   The fifteen knights were so astounded by him that they stopped eating to watch what he was doing; and they did not care for such a situation, since he was eating against their wishes.

The chief of them, who possessed a certain perverse courtliness, said to them: 'Don't worry: just let him eat as much as wants; then, when he's had his fill, I fancy he'll settle his account with us. By the faith I owe you, when he gets up from this meal, he'll never take away with him anything worth so much as a whiting. It was unlucky for him that he came to sit with us in our group. It would have been better for him to be at Dinant!' Fergus hears them, but gave no hint or sign of it. He ate the whole of his loaf and then went quickly to grab another one. That they were not prepared to let him do, but all said with one accord: 'You're a great glutton, sir vassal! You were never called when this meal was served, but now you make yourself chief steward of it! May it be with the living fiend's blessing that you're making so free with it! You'll certainly pay for it all before you leave here!'

3342   'My lords,' says he, 'I've never heard anything like it! It seems to me you're making a mistake: I haven't finished eating, and you're already reckoning up the bill! The custom of my country is this: when people have sat down to a meal, share and share alike, they first of all eat as much as they feel like and then reckon up afterwards. I'm not asking to take away anything of yours, as God's my witness. I've a fine silk tunic I'll give you to cover the cost.' – 'A curse on anyone with that idea!' say the robbers in unison. 'By the true holy Cross on which God Himself was stretched, you'll not get away with either your lance or your shield! You'll even leave for us that good steed tethered outside there, and won't ever take that any further!'

3362   He hears them threatening him and jumps angrily forward. He catches up the spit with all the capons and strikes and thwacks the first he encounters to such effect that he knocks both eyes out of his head. The others leap up as fast as they can and surround him on all sides. It was sheer folly for him to have launched himself at them unless he can defend himself. He has to be very much on the alert, because they make a violent attack on him. He draws his keen sword and defends himself like a lion. He took many a blow from sticks and the wood in the hearth; but

they were repaid to their cost, just as they deserved. He proffered
them his sword to good purpose, for of those fifteen knights only
two remained unscathed, whilst he slew the other thirteen.

3384 Those two fell to their knees to seek and beg for mercy.
However, they may not find it but will be killed by him on the
spot, unless they go to give themselves up to King Arthur and put
themselves at his disposal. They swore and pledged him their
word to go there willingly and on his behalf to greet the king
along with all the nobility, and never in all their lives to commit
any further theft. With that they set out on their way, and Fergus
leaves them at the bower. Nightfall was not far away, and the sun
was setting. Beside a pine-tree near a copse Fergus stopped and
dismounted, then lay down under the pine; and there he slept a
little, for he was tired from his travels and from carrying his
equipment. He rested there that night until, in the morning, the
sun rose and dispersed the dew.

3410 That morning the king had assembled his barons to ask and
seek advice on how, by what plan and with what power, he might
take vengeance on that knight who had caused them so much
trouble. They all remain silent and mute: not one of them is so
bold or proud as to dare take up his equipment or don his armour
in order to go and do battle for the wimple. All keep quiet on
every hand except for Sir Kay, the seneschal. He then said, in a
voice loud enough for the king to hear, if he chose to: 'Sire,
there's no need for you to be dismayed: at least the new knight*
you dubbed the other evening will hand him over to you – I'm
sure of that, for he promised he would!'

3430 When my lord Gawain hears Kay mocking and deriding him,
he gives a slight sardonic smile before telling him very angrily:
'You talk too much just to amuse people, terrible tattler that you
are. If the emperor took my advice, you'd always carry a fiddle
from now on: at least you'd serve him with that when my lord
held his court. Then each of us would give you a cloak or mantle
for your service!' On hearing the altercation between lord
Gawain and Kay, the king said: 'Sir, by the faith I owe you, this

isn't the place to squabble when you should be advising me. Stop these insults! My lord Kay's in the habit of saying and telling things that no one else would dream of. Through his mockery he has robbed me of many an excellent, distinguished knight; but I don't want to have a quarrel with him, so I beg you to drop the matter.'

3455   As the king was speaking these words and rebuking his nephew, he sees coming through the gate the Black Knight carrying the horn and silk wimple; and he says: 'Dear nephew, as God's my witness, we'll soon have some news, either bad or good. I can see an armed man approaching, covered in fresh blood, who doesn't seem to me in a very fit state. His shield is completely knocked to pieces. I'm very curious to know the meaning of this. – But it seems to me he's holding in his right hand a wimple and a horn; and he has his shield at his neck. I think it's the young gentleman who was made a new knight the other day after the feast of Saint John when I arrived from Cardigan. What do you say, my dear nephew Gawain?' – 'Sire,' he replies, 'by Saint Germain, that's not he: in my opinion it looks more like the Black Knight who has killed your noblemen. But in a while you'll know better who he is, where he's from and what he's come for. We'll hear the truth of the matter.'

3483   Then the knight dismounts. His shield, though, hangs in fragments, his hauberk is burst open and his bare sides can be seen through it, and his helmet is shattered, because Fergus has been to work on it. Fully armed, the Black Knight mounts the steps to the great hall in fear and trembling, for he feels extremely guilty. Nevertheless, he proceeded straight to where good King Arthur was sitting, leaning against one of his barons. He begins to speak up so that he is heard by fools and wise men alike. He greets the king and his nobles in the name of the Lord God in Heaven – everybody except for Kay the seneschal: he ignored him completely, according to his instructions.

3503   He then said to the king: 'Hear me, good sire! I am sent to your court, this you should know, by a young gentleman – the most courtly and handsome, the most gallant and valiant who could be found anywhere. I don't know who he is, never having seen him before, except that I heard him called Fergus. He has sent you this horn by me. I'm that miserable wretch who, against my will, have had the dire misfortune to be vanquished by him in arms, overcome and captured. I am the man who has wronged you so grievously: I can't deny it. I come to surrender as your prisoner. You can, if you wish, treat me in any way you like: have me suffer pain and torture, be burnt or strung up in the wind, or inflict any greater punishment, if you know one. But, by my soul, Fergus sends word begging you, dear kind sir, for love of him to forgive me for causing your great wrath: and when he sent me here he fully assured me that you would do so. See: here are the horn and wimple. I present them to you on his behalf and place myself at your mercy; for I pledged him on my oath to do so, and I certainly don't want to break my word. I've only one death to die!'

3535   The king, hearing and understanding the message that he can do just as he wishes with that knight, burning, drowning, hanging or mangling him, began to reflect a little and sought advice on the subject from his faithful intimate, my lord Gawain. He, a noble man with only the best of intentions, recommends him to show generosity and pardon the knight for the anger he caused. What advantage would he get by killing him? He would not in that way have back those who were slain. The dead to the dead, the living to the living!* Then the leading nobles who hear this think highly of the advice and support it, saying that is a good course to take; and it should not displease the king if he wishes to join his company. My lord Gawain pleads urgently with him to agree, as do all the others. The king at once forgives him for his wrongdoing, the cause of all his anger, since his barons urge him to do so. Here now is the knight more happy, glad, joyful and delighted than ever before in his life. Joy makes him forget his grief and the discomfort from his wound. Without the least trepidation he sits down at the king's feet. He finds many who ask him and enquire what happened to the one who fought with him; but he has no information he can give them. At this the king is sad and depressed, and so too are all the others. They are extremely upset that he has not returned to the court. Every single one of them is disconsolate.

3577   While they were speaking in this fashion and giving the knight a warm welcome, the man who had been in the fight in the desolate forest dismounted at the block and with him his mistress and the dwarf. Immediately they make their way to the high tables, where the king is sitting. The knight recounted his adventure. There was not the least noise or murmuring: instead they all listened attentively to what he related, telling them how Fergus had defeated him and beaten and railed at his dwarf in front of his tent. Then he said that he had pledged his victor to give himself up to King Arthur, and this he does most willingly. The king said to him: 'My dear friend, you'll never suffer shame or trouble here. Just for the love of the man on whose behalf you speak, I am most anxious for you to be honoured to your satisfaction in my court.'

3602   Looking ahead, he sees the others coming with their helmets laced. The king and all his people are utterly amazed, for they correctly assumed that they are sent to court by Fergus. High and low, they are quite astonished that he wields such great power. Then they all say that without doubt he is the best knight ever to mount a charger: such is the praise he receives from all the noblemen. The newcomers did not pause before they arrived in front of the king. Then, each speaking for himself, they assert that not in the entire world does so much chivalry and vigour abound in a single knight as in the one who vanquished them. The king is very sad and dejected; and, but for the fear of being thought childish, he would there and then have tackled Kay who, by his outrageously scurrilous talk, has robbed him of the most gallant man who ever bore arms or shield. He did not, however, want to start a quarrel, since he was very afraid of behaving unworthily; so with difficulty he restrained himself. With great generosity he retained all the knights with him. But he desperately regrets the absence of Fergus, whom he is unable to forget. If he thought he could find him anywhere, you may be certain he would go there either on his own or with a great company. But his efforts would be in vain, because he would not find him for a very long time. We shall not tell you any more about King Arthur or his barons: instead I shall return to my main subject at the point where I left it.

3643   The next morning was very bright. Fergus lay beneath the pine tree, having slept for a very long time because he was extremely exhausted and weary from the hardships he had suffered. So he was happy to sleep right up to six o'clock, for he found it very restful there. Then he roused and woke up, took his arms and mounted his good, handsome steed, and resumed his journey. *For an entire year Fergus endured such grief, care and misfortune that he never ate any bread or cooked meat, for he had none. But when he was tormented by great hunger, he would hunt until he caught some buck or roe-deer, and then ate its flesh quite raw, like a dog. His face was thin and hairy, as he was unshaven and his head unshorn; and the tunic he wore was torn and tattered. The hauberk beat against his bare sides, which were skinny and emaciated. He was quite wasted away and famished, as too was his horse, for he had had many a rough lodging.

3673   A year and more had already passed when Fergus was riding through the most beautiful and leafy woodland seen by any man since the first was created by God. In those woods was a spring whose water flowed towards the east. I am sure there is none more lovely this side of Christ's birthplace. And it had been given a property possessed by no other spring; for there will be no man so sick or ailing that, if he drinks of it, he will not be fit again. Fergus came to that spring, which ran very clear and pure, not because he was looking for it, but because Fortune sent him there, wishing to cure him of the ills she had made him endure. For a long while she had been hostile to him, but now treats him gently and kindly. Fortune wishes to lift him up as high as she can raise him.

3697   Fergus gazes at the beautiful water, which flows up onto an
        elevated strand composed of precious stones: they were very
        attractive and of great worth and beauty in their many different
        ways; and there is no precious stone on earth that was not found
        beside that small spring. On the bank was a chapel built in days
        gone by. It was guarded night and day by a dwarf who, without a
        word of a lie, foretold the future to those who passed by and
        drank of the spring. But should anyone travel that way without
        drinking or tasting the water flowing from the spring, he would
        not tell him a single thing, however much he might question him.
        Fergus watches the water swirling and washing to and fro.
        Because of its beauty he had the desire to drink just a little of it.
        Alighting from his steed, he came to the water and drank from
        his hand as much of it as he wished. The moment he tasted it he
        regained all his spiritual and mental force, his strength and his
        boldness. Now he was glad, happy and full of joy, lighter and
        more nimble than a merlin and fiercer than a lion. He completely
        forgot his care, roundly asserting and swearing instead that there
        is no knight in the world to whom he would not give a hard fight,
        should he take it into his head to set upon him.

3736   Thereupon the dwarf came out of the chapel and, recognis-
        ing him, said, 'Noble knight, son of the peasant of Pelande, may
        things go well with you! Joy and gladness and great honour
        await you, that I declare. I know you better than you me, and am
        well aware that you are in quest of the admirable Galiene, to
        whom you refused your love. You will have suffered and endured
        many a trial and many troubles, much rain and many storms
        and have had to take many a blow before you may have her back
        again. But of this you may be sure: you will learn from me the
        way in which you will obtain her. *If you are gallant and clever
        enough and have sufficient valour to be prepared to go to
        Dunnottar to obtain the shining shield guarded by the hairy
        hag, then you may still have your beloved. If you are unwilling to
        undertake this onerous task, then expend no more of your
        efforts on her account!' When Fergus heard what the dwarf said,

he was beside himself with joy. He supposes and concludes that
the dwarf is a supernatural creature; so he is very happy to listen
to what this dwarf has to tell him about recovering his sweetheart. Had anyone given him the whole of Pavia, he would not
have increased his joy.

3770   However, wanting to know how best to get her back and
whereabouts he could find her, he said to the dwarf: 'Little fellow,
by the faith you owe the Holy Spirit, since you say, and I believe
you, that you know me better than I you and have addressed me
by name, if you are willing tell me here and now the place where
I can find her; for there's nothing I long for so much. If the Lord
God were pleased to take me to Himself and pardon all the
misdeeds I ever committed against Him, and if the bright-faced
Galiene were in the darkness of Hell, then I should go there: for
love of her I'd leave Paradise above to join her down below and
suffer pain, hardship and torment until the great Judgement
Day.* You'll do well to give me that information. As you know
my decision, and I don't ask for anything else, you really should
tell me, and then I'll be your liegeman for all my living days!'

3799   The dwarf answers him: 'Knight, I could very easily direct you
as you ask me to; but you may be sure you will not have her as
easily as you think. There will be piercing of shields carried out in
situations of mortal peril before you can have the comfort, joy and
delight of the one who is the object of your concern. I tell you for
certain, without evasion, that whoever wants to achieve success
must pay for it. And before you have it, you will truly pay a very
high price for it, and not in gold or silver but, you understand,
with your own person. Yet whatever wound you may receive, you
will never lose a drop of your blood: fight in safety, if you can find
the occasion. You will need to show great prowess if you ever wish
to have her. You will obtain her through deeds of valour. You
cannot indeed achieve her by payments or gifts, nor by courage or
by force unless you have the splendid shield that hangs inside
Dunnottar's tower: you will not have her otherwise through any
advice of mine.' When he hears he will not have his sweetheart

back unless he has that shield, he tells the dwarf that he will get it if it is ever to be had by any man. But he wants to know further what the power of that shield is and where it is to be found.

3837   The dwarf at once replied: 'The shield has such power that whoever has it in his possession will never lose his life in armed conflict nor be unhorsed by any mortal man alive. It has another property too: that the night will never be so dark that the tower where the shield is being kept is not surrounded by a bright radiance, as much by night as by day. I can tell you that if the whole of the English army were gathered and had sworn your death, but you had the sole advantage of being in that tower having raised the drawbridge, you would be in no fear of them all, provided you had a supply of food. That tower is perched on a rock, round which beats the sea. One goes in by a gate, there being only one entrance; but that has a serious encumbrance, for an old woman (may a demon burn her!) guards the gate and turret so that no one dares approach. She holds a steel scythe a foot and a half across. There is under heaven no man so well armoured and no knight so bold that, if the hag caught him a blow, she would not slice him through the trunk. That is the guardian the shield has.

3871   'If you definitely want to have it, there will be a fight between the two of you which you will find very hard, never in your life having been through one like it; and you will never have experienced such great fear as you will feel that day when you two meet in combat. I can assure you it will be no sport like the quintain or a tournament: the hag is extremely aggressive. By the end of the contest, the splendid shield will certainly be yours. Now do the best you can, for you'll have no other news of your lovely sweetheart from me!' With that he goes into the chapel. Fergus follows on his heels; but an iron door shut in his face, entirely by itself. He knocked and beat on it for a long time, calling on the dwarf to let him in, for he has something more to say to him. He is very distressed to be refused. Then, seeing he will get no further, he mounts his horse, which was tethered at the bridge.

3897   Fergus rides through the woodland. He has turned all his thoughts and mind to knightly deeds, yet without forgetting his noble and prudent sweetheart. Love brings him some consolation, and you may be sure his love is great.* Now his anguish is tempered, since he knows she is not dead. He is comforted by his high hope and by the dwarf's assurance that by virtue of the shield he would recover her for whom he had longed so much. He goes riding through the countryside, covering much ground each day and passing through many regions, sheltering for the night in many places. But there would seem to me no profit in detailing for you all the places where he found a lodging. He crosses the entire region of which his beloved is the acknowledged mistress without either of them becoming aware of it by hearsay. He travelled continually, asking for information as to where he would find that shield; but no one in the district knows. He has placed his whole reliance on Fortune to guide him safely where she pleases. Having passed through the whole of Lothian, he took lodging in a place known as Maiden Castle,* where he thought he would hear news of the shield he is seeking. But nobody living in the stronghold gave him the slightest information about it.

3934   *In the morning he left that fortress and came to the port by the sea which I have heard many people call Queensferry. That is where Lothian ends; and beyond lies Scotland, with the sea separating these two lands. Fergus embarked on a barge which he found there at the crossing point all ready to leave. Having taken his horse aboard, he said to the boatmen that he would be happy to pay the dues before he left the vessel. Wicked rogues that they were, they took it into their heads that, once on the open sea, they would drown him in the water and have all his equipment. There were ten of the boatmen and none so treacherous, I fancy, in the whole kingdom of England. They are wanting to start an affray, which will before long turn out most grievously and painfully for them.

3959   The wind blows up in the rigging, and very soon they are at sea. Then they begin to consider how they will be able to deal with

the knight who is with them. They resolve that, should he put up
any defence at all, they will kill him at once with the poles and
oars. Fergus has fallen in with some wicked scoundrels, and he
had better be gallant and agile: a fate is being proposed for him
which will prove very disastrous unless the Lord God on high
lends him aid and succour. It was unlucky for him that he had
dealings with their band!

3975   The leader said to the young man: 'My good friend, pay for
your charger's passage and your own. There's nothing for us to
discuss: I don't care much for earnings that have to be haggled
over! If you'd now reached that bank, you'd never pay us
anything, but go off without a "by your leave" or any payment.
You'll do well to settle your debt, for I don't see any more
sensible course.' Then Fergus comes to realise that they are
wicked criminals, which, you may be sure, distresses him
greatly. If he were on land, I suppose he would make very light
of the lot of them; but on the sea, not knowing how to proceed,
he takes good care not to give any offensive reply. Instead he
said in a very prudent, courteous tone: 'My good boatmen, as
God's my witness, I have no money with me; but I'll be very
happy to give you the tunic on my back, for I do intend to
settle up with you.' The leader, set on trouble, arrogantly
replies: 'Fellow, you look like a rascal to me! Am I now to go
and set my sails just to trade a silk tunic? Now I've really learnt
something! You'll certainly pay us very well before you leave
this ship, or else you'll leave your security behind! I've no time
for your insolence. You might say something to me that would
soon have you drinking more than your fill!'

4012   Then, hearing himself threatened, Fergus was beside himself
with rage. Whoever had seen him fit his good, strong, heavy
shield to his arm and put on the bravest face possible for a man
fallen among his mortal enemies would have been deeply
impressed! If there is anyone now who dares make a move to take
or touch him, he will never be able to retreat again. The leader
begins to shout: 'Hit him, hit him, my boatmen! He'll certainly

not get out of this!' Then they rain blows from all sides, landing them thick and fast on the rim of his shield, his body and his flanks. He is almost battered down, for the traitors press him hard. In the end they pay very dearly for it, because his steel sword is in his hand. Time and again he has them make its acquaintance; and anyone he catches fairly and squarely with it cannot escape without some injury: he cleaves them right down to the feet! He has so wounded nine of them that they cannot harm him or be of any assistance. He goes to do business with the leader who had started this affray; but that is not to the man's liking: instead he lets go of the tiller and jumps into the sea, preferring to die rather than be killed. Fergus seizes the tiller and steers the drifting boat. The wind, lashing the rigging and masts, sends it scudding along. On the further side he made a landfall below an outlandish castle called Dunfermline.* There Fergus went ashore and mounted his horse, leaving the barge to drift.

4056   He goes riding through Scotland as Fortune leads him. He rode about that region for two months and a week without ever hearing any report of either the shield or the tower until it happened one day that, under Fortune's guidance, he saw and recognised the radiance as promised him by the dwarf. Then he knew for sure that this was the object of his search. He proceeds towards the tower, and the nearer he gets the more pleased he is. The shield emits a radiance second only to the bright sun's. In all the world there is no clerk clever enough to record in his lifetime a tenth part of the beauty possessed by the fine shield. Had I now devoted my full attention to giving a description or account, I could find nothing better to say of its beauty than what I know of it from having found it in writing. You may take it as a fact that no man in this mortal world can look at it any more than he could at the summer sun at noon. I am very amazed at one thing, namely that the man who made it was not blinded when he saw such a brilliance at close quarters, unless he was a supernatural creature. The great light delights Fergus and will please him all the more when he sees the shield from nearer at hand.

4093   At full gallop on a slack rein he came to a causeway leading
to the tower.* He saw standing on the bridge the hideous, shaggy
old woman with the scythe at the ready on her shoulder. She
had long, plaited whiskers, and her eyes were two feet apart,
whilst her teeth were yellowish-brown, broad and pointed. She
had the appearance of a fiend or demon. As soon as Fergus came
into sight, she began to hiss loudly and make a show of very
great joy, for she expected to have him very quickly mangled or
killed. Seeing her, Fergus is extremely thoughtful. He goes at full
speed in her direction. The hag had raised her head and
proceeded to knit her brows. When she saw him approaching
her, she braced herself on the bridge, so that it almost gave way
completely under her feet. Fergus rides on, spurring hard. But he
was unable to go in on horseback, since the entrance had been
made so narrow that only a single man could pass. When he sees
he will have to fight the hag on foot, Fergus is highly annoyed,
put out and sorry. Nevertheless, he dismounts from his horse
and ties it to a willow.

4126   The hag then comes leaping forward with the intention of
denying him entrance. But she had the idea too late now that he
has already advanced more than eight yards up the bridge. She is
convinced that with her very first blows she will have killed him
on the spot. However, he is not so slow-witted or stupid that he
cannot dodge when he sees the blow coming. They do not spend
long in getting acquainted, and their conversation is very brief!
Without any speech or challenge, Fergus hurls his stout lance at
her with great vigour and force. The hag is unable to evade it,
and it pins her through the flanks, at which she trumpets like an
elephant, and her voice carries over a full league's distance. The
hag feels herself wounded and sees the bridge around her gory
with blood running from her wound. Yet she is not in the least
dismayed, but furiously lets fly with that sharp scythe of hers,
catching him on the shining helmet. As easily as one might cut
off a twig she split and shattered it right down to the skull-cap.
Had she caught him lower down, he would never have had any

use for a doctor, and would have played no future part in conducting a battle or tournament! He knows and sees quite evidently
that she is not sparing him at all; and he is in great fear of her.

4165 But the hag does not linger. She deals him a mighty blow on
his shield, cutting it in half; and had Fergus not dodged, she
would have sliced him through his flanks, which would have been
a tragic shame. Fergus leaps aside, very afraid of this hag, who
has no love for him at all. However, she is half lost, because she
has sunk the scythe into a pillar of dark brown marble that was
set on the bridge, so that she cannot pull it out again. She does,
though, tug so hard that she rocks both pillar and bridge. Now
Fergus sees something that gives him satisfaction, pleasure and
delight. If he does not now launch a strong attack on her, he will
not think himself worth two hawthorn berries. He draws from
its sheath the keen-edged sword, then makes for her and cuts off
at the wrists both her hands, with which she was holding the
scythe. Now he is less nervous of fighting the great, loathsome
hag. When she sees she is lost and her strength has left her, she
turns back in flight towards the tower so as still to save her life.
Grasping the shining sword, Fergus pursues her hotly. With the
sharp sword he dealt the giantess an amazingly hard blow, catching her full on the point where the stomach joins the chest, that
is below the breast, so that he cleaves through flesh, bone and
guts; and down she fell.

4204 This turn of events pleases Fergus more than any of his earlier
adventures, for he supposes that he will be able to have the shield
at once, without any delay. However, he will meet with very stout
opposition before he has free possession of it. Round the shield
there lies a dragon a good eighteen or more feet long: its body
was fully eight feet, its tail six, and its head four feet long – an
exceedingly foul creature bigger than the one slain by Tristan,
Mark's nephew. Now Fergus is happy and delighted; but his
mood will quickly change before night has fallen and before he
has obtained the shield. He climbs up through the gate, leaving
the hag dead and having no further worry about her.

4224   Looking ahead, he could see the great hall as brightly lit as if
        it had been set ablaze, though he does not yet see the shield. He
        went straight through the hall and came into a courtyard more
        attractive and splendid than was to be found in any city or
        stronghold. There the good shield hangs at the top of a marble
        pillar, and there the dragon lurks beneath the trees. There are
        nine well-hewn steps built quite high in an orderly arrangement.
        The person wishing to obtain the shield has to climb these steps.
        Fergus gazes at that wonder, which does not have its equal nor
        ever will have. He thinks he can have it quite peaceably and that
        he will not find it contested any more. The brilliance has so
        dazzled him that he hears little and does not see that great
        serpent, which was asleep, as God had ordained: that was a true
        miracle! So he continued up the steps and took by its straps the
        splendid, radiant shield. But he committed one grave indiscretion,
        by lingering there.

4254   He takes pleasure and delight in the shield, because he sees
        how beautiful and strong it is and because he need have no fear
        of death so long as he carries it in battle; but he feels even greater
        joy because of his understanding and belief that through the
        shield he would recover her whom he loved faithfully. He comes
        down the steps more impetuously than he should, and treads on
        the beam under which the dragon is sleeping. The beam hits it on
        the ear; and it springs up in an instant, and far more frighten-
        ingly than usual. Then, seeing that the knight had robbed it of
        the object it was guarding, it spouts fire and flame from its jaws
        at him with such force that, had it not been for the splendid
        shield, it would have burnt and roasted him to cinders. But the
        Lord God protected him from suffering any harm or distress,
        except from the stench alone.

4279   Fergus draws his good sword. The dragon advances, jaws
        agape, pouncing like a living demon and gnashing its teeth
        together. There is no man who, seeing it, would have dared stay
        there, except for the one who, with valiant and bold heart, waited
        there for it: no one should be compared with him. The dragon

leaps headlong at him, giving him with its tail a great blow that makes the shield ring; but it is hard to shatter. Fergus flies against a pillar, which he hits with such force that his heart nearly had to leave his breast for the agony. The dragon breaks and tears apart the tree where the shield had been hanging, twisting about more rapidly than a snake. Fergus was very put out by the whole business and, you may be sure, very annoyed. Any other would have taken to his heels; but he would prefer to die with honour than live dishonourably and be a subject of reproach for it. Blood spurts from his mouth, ears and nose, so that he is completely covered in it. Then, when he sees the blood spattering his bright hauberk, he is so distressed that he almost collapses. He raises the shield aloft, then, raging like a lion, strikes the dragon a mighty blow with his sword on its scaly haunch, slicing across its head and half through its neck.*

4318   Had anyone now given him the lordship of England as a fief, he would not have been a tenth as jubilant and happy. He does not remember his distress and pain from striking the pillar: he entirely forgets his great anguish. The dragon writhes and twists and thrashes its tail about, laying low everything it hits. Fergus draws away a little, being quite convinced that it does not have the strength to get up to do him any harm or hurt. Now it is dead, to Fergus' delight. He goes searching through the fortress to see if he could find anyone who would challenge him for the shield; but he does not find a living thing. For just a short while he rests, because he is very weary. But rather than wait there long, he went down over the bridge to find his good horse in the place where he had left it. Then he sets his feet in the stirrups and leaves Dunnottar Castle, carrying with him the splendid shield. With him he takes his renown and valour. He bears with him too courage, strength and vigour, for which truly he will be feared and dreaded.

4351   Fergus goes off rejoicing, from time to time fitting the shield to his arm and flourishing it as though in the presence of someone wanting to fight him. He entered a forest and went riding onwards until he had a stroke of fortune which pleased and suited him. Just where he came to the sea he found a large vessel belonging to a worthy, courteous and knowledgeable merchant. He had ten boats there laden with leather, which he had bought in that country. He was only waiting for the wind to get up in order to leave the land. Fergus was not nervous, but greeted the men in the big ship in the name of Him who created the world. Then he begged them to let him pay for a crossing with them: he will make no fuss about giving them whatever they would like to charge him. The merchant was a very sensible man; and, thinking this was a supernatural being asking him to be ferried across, said: 'That won't be refused you, my dear good friend. Come along! I ask you for no payment other than just the honour of your acquaintance.' He at once lowers the gangway for him; and he goes aboard, fully armed. The shield throws out a great radiance, to the alarm of all those in the ship. Fergus gives them his reassurance that they have no need to fear: they can be quite confident. The wind at once rises from the north and bears them away at a good speed. It was still barely evening when they made land on the other side, at Queensferry in fact.

4394   He stayed with them all that night until, early the following morning, he set out on his road. And so, having left the merchants, he journeyed all day, encountering no man or woman. Nor did he drink or eat, but was not in the least dismayed: that had often been his lot since he undertook this journey. On a hillside next to a river-bank he sees three shepherds guarding their animals. He galloped up to them and asked them for information about this country: what was the name of the district he was in and who governed it. They give him the truthful reply that from ancient times this country has been called Lothian, and it is ruled by a lady, certainly the noblest character ever born of mother; and her name is Galiene.

4419   However, a powerful king is waging war on her and laying siege, with his great company of nobles, to the fortress of Roxburgh. He had beggared her men and laid waste her fiefs,

burnt her towns, villages and cities so that nothing worth a cherry
remains outside the castle where she is besieged. And she is worse
served by those traitors who have abandoned her because of this,
so that I believe she has no man with her to give her support other
than thirty armed knights, having had all the rest slain in the
attacks launched by those outside. And those within will not hold
the castle much longer, for they have no wine or wheat for their
subsistence. Before a fortnight is up, they will have to surrender.
When Fergus heard of the devastation wrought on his dear sweetheart by her opponent, he was full of wrath and fury. He will, if
possible, go to her aid before two more days have passed. He
immediately leaves the shepherds and rides on by the woodland,
for part of the time rejoicing to have located his beloved, but not
at all pleased at that man having shut her up in the castle. He
would not have wished that for anything, and would rather die
than fail to harry the man who is laying her land waste.*

4455   Fergus rides on rapt in these thoughts and sighing for his
sweetheart. He intends to make straight for the siege; but one
road deceives him, for his attention wanders. *He leaves his
route and takes another road, which leads him to the Dolorous
Mount. There he will have a perilous lodging unless he is able to
defend himself. He will need to speak with the wicked giant of
Melrose Mountain, who had there constructed and enclosed a
wonderfully powerful stronghold, below which was a great,
amazingly deep gorge. Fergus approaches the bridge, where he
will take many a blow. It was already almost evening when he arrived
at the mountain and the fortress with its redoubtable keep sited
on the slope of a rock. He would like to go to lodge in the castle
to get some rest. It would have been better for him to go on.
Before he made much progress at all, he sees the giant on the
bridge, holding in his hand a little stick! – There is no man this
side of Barletta who would not have been well laden if he had
that on his shoulder! The club was huge and massive, the giant
wicked and cruel: Fergus will have rough hospitality if that giant
can manage it!

4488   When he sees the blazing light of the shield hanging at Fergus'
        neck, he immediately recognises it and knows well enough that
        this knight had killed his wife, who was the shield's guardian. He
        feels grief and anger in his heart and almost goes mad with rage.
        Now Fergus will need to have his wits about him to be on his
        guard and put up a good defence; for this swashbuckler will
        want, if he can, to avenge in the very near future the death of his
        wife and the dragon and get his hands on the shield. These,
        however, are very foolish thoughts of his, because no one will
        ever have the shield other than the person who has it at this
        moment. The giant was both wicked and stupid. He comes leap-
        ing and bounding at Fergus, his club up on his shoulder, and
        says: 'You miserable wretch! Just put that down at once, because
        you certainly have no right to it; and since you've taken it over,
        you'll pay very dear for it!' Fergus said: 'Damn that! You were
        quite safe when I won it and overcame the hag and killed the
        dragon: you never gave me any help, and now you want a share in
        the shield! In the Devil's name, bad luck on the one who brought
        it here, if he meekly leaves it with you like that! Look out for
        yourself: I challenge you!'

4523   He then spurs his speedy horse. The edges of his fine steel
        sword were very sharp. He sends it fishing into his body, so that
        it goes straight through. The giant does not halt his rush at
        Fergus, but beats and bludgeons him with his club just as hard as
        he is able. I really believe that if anyone delivered such blows
        against a wall, he would, in my judgment, knock down a large
        part of it. Nor, for his part, does Fergus spare him, but, having
        drawn his polished sword, strikes mighty blows with it in the
        struggle. Yet Fergus would not have lasted long against that
        demon were it not for God not wishing the giant to kill him and
        Fortune protecting him. The devil bleeds profusely. In his rage
        and fury he launches with his applewood club a great blow on
        the quartered shield, aiming to break and smash it and crush the
        knight. But he does not break or shatter it. The blow is deflected
        over the saddle onto the horse's neck: its neck and head are

beaten down, and it falls to the ground. The fight between these two will be on foot, if they want to keep it up.

4556 Now Fergus really thinks he will die of grief when he sees the horse slaughtered which his father had given him when he set out. You can be sure he had no friendly feelings for the donor of that favour! With the steel sword he was wielding he thrust from a distance at the giant and cut off his right fist. If only you had seen how furious he grew! He dashes at him with his left fist, which he brings down on him with all the strength in his arm, bursting and snapping all the laces on his helmet, so that it flies down to his feet; and the giant goes and seizes it. Fergus has nothing to cover himself with other than the coif and the shield. Now he knows well that if his fellow combatant can retrieve his club, his blows will be irresistible, because he does not spare him. Fergus wants to deny him the recovery of the club, so, with his keen naked sword, he comes running to where he sees the club lying, and there waits for the giant's attack. He delivers it with a fierce ardour. With his massive, sturdy arm he caught the shining hauberk, tearing, ripping and rending it as if it were a piece of Syrian cloth. He left the whole hauberk in tatters.

4590 No one should be surprised if Fergus was afraid. Now he is in dire need of the shield's protection; for he has lost the use of his helmet, and the hauberk he was wearing had, I fancy, no part intact but the coif and the shoulder-pieces. The combat was unequal, for the other is taller than Fergus by a full four feet and more and is immensely burly and strong. But he had no more courage, heart or valour than the man standing against him. The fight is hard and bitter; but it goes ill for the traitor, the low villain. The blood flows in streams from both his sides; and his arrogance is somewhat subdued, whilst he is more apprehensive than usual. Fergus clearly notices this and launches another attack on him. The giant did not dodge, but came furiously at him in turn. Fergus puts all his effort and power into dealing him a very fine blow: on his right-hand side he severs the shoulder from the trunk. The giant roars and yells and shouts as if he were a living demon. Burning with rage, he runs at Fergus and seizes him in his left arm. He races down the rock, carrying the knight with the firm intention of drowning him in the rushing, thundering river running below the castle. He really thinks he can be rid of him that way, provided that he can carry him as far as the bridge. But, summoning all his energy, Fergus wrenches his sword from him: he puts so much strength and effort into this that he almost runs out of breath. The giant, meanwhile, lifts him up and squeezes him. Cleverly Fergus thrusts the sword into him below his breast, slicing his heart to pieces; and he falls to the ground with a great clatter. Had an oak-tree been toppled, it would not have made such a crash.*

4642   When Fergus was out of the clutches of the giant he had slain, he was not too perturbed. Seeing himself free from the giant, he enters the castle unhindered, since no one refuses him entry. Up in the main paved hall he finds two maidens sitting, making a great show of grief on account of two knights, their lovers, whom the giant had slain at sundown the previous evening. The son of the foul devil is having himself massaged by them. Fergus seizes him by the hair and with his fist gives him such a violent punch that he makes his eyes pop out of his forehead, and he falls unconscious. Hauling and dragging him right down the stairs, Fergus hurls him into the depths of the moat: he has rid the country of him!

4664   Both the maidens fall in tears at his feet, saying that they will henceforth serve him all their days if he delivers them from the life of shame to which they were destined. Seeing them so grief-stricken, Fergus feels great pity for them. He raises them up and asks them if there is anyone but themselves in the keep. They tell him: 'No sir, we are alone, and there is nobody else here other than just you yourself.' This delights Fergus. He ordered one of them to go and close the gate; and he would go into the apartments to make sure there was nothing there which could do him any harm or mischief. He searches through them high and low.

4684   He goes into an out-of-the-way cellar and finds, in a stall, a
horse of which I intend to tell you no lie: there was none so handsome, swifter or more fleet-footed in England, nor one to give a
knight a better ride. The giant had kept and tended it very well
for two and a half years in that cellar, from which it never
emerged for any man, squire or stable-lad, except just for the
giant alone. The horse was handsome and well-fleshed. Fergus at
once walks up to it with the intention of stroking it. The horse
begins to snort, buck, paw the ground, and kick out with its back
hooves, making the stone floor resound. Fergus is very astonished to find the horse behaving in this way because it does not
know him at all, since no one other than just that devil used to
handle it. The horse shies and jibs violently as if it wanted to
avenge the death of the giant, its master. Fergus finds an apple-
wood stick lying at his feet and picks it up. Going straight to the
horse, he hits it so hard on the forehead that he knocks it flat. He
strikes it again and again on the flanks: never was a horse better
broken in than this one was tamed by Fergus with that massive
apple-wood stick! The horse remained lying down for a long
time. Fergus took hold of it by the reins, which were of silver, and
up it jumped. But he did not find it as frisky as it had been before,
so well indeed had he tamed it. Seeing that, Fergus remarks,
having a good laugh to himself: 'It's best to tame a rogue before
he has the ability to rebel.' The horse gave a prance and a neigh.

4730   With that, Fergus comes out of the cellar, leaving the charger
in the stall. Having returned to the main hall, he has himself
disarmed by the ladies and his shield, which he loves and cher-
ishes, taken into a separate room. But now he is in great need of
their good offices, being badly hurt and injured in his body,
although there is no sign of a wound on the surface. The maidens tend and serve him as best they can that evening, and bring
him a meal. That task was not too difficult for them: there was
plenty of wine, bread and sides of bacon. Hanging from the
pillars in the keep were more than a thousand shields, hauberks,
helmets, and all the gear for arming a knight. The giant had

amassed too silken cloths and precious fabrics with wheel-motifs: with all this the Castle of the Dark Rock was well supplied. Now Fergus has a good and choice lodging, completely to his taste. From there he will be able boldly to make a fair bid to rescue his sweetheart, who stands in great need of help.

4759   They then sat down to supper, with the maidens hurrying to bring him warm water in pure gold basins and to serve the food. Then they ate, just the three of them. When he had eaten enough, Fergus, having no further needs, goes to lie down in a bed. It was a fine, soft one, and he promptly fell asleep. But the ladies are not idle. Long before daybreak they provided for him a splendid, excellent bath, all prepared and just the thing for relieving aches and pains. Very early in the morning they had him get into it. Most lovingly these maidens serve him as their lord, attending to everything they can. One of them goes to make ready a shirt and breeches of fine linen whiter than April flowers. For three days he was in that castle; and in truth there was none of them on which he was not bathed, until he was quite fit and healthy.

4785   One day he climbed to the upper floor and put his head out of the windows. He can see the tilled and the uncultivated land and, all round, the country and territory of Lothian. And quite clearly he sees Roxburgh,* where his beloved is besieged. He sees shelters, pavilions, tents and awnings outside the town: more than thirty thousand of them. He sees the land burnt and laid waste, which displeases more than delights him! Now he will think himself a great coward if they maintain that siege undisturbed for long without his investigating them. He immediately leaves the upper floor, goes down the staircase in the keep and comes running into the hall. Seeing him come, the maidens are not backward in serving him.

4805   Fergus tells them everything, describing the affliction and deep shame imposed by that man on his beloved. But if he does not now take the offensive against him, he will have a very low opinion of himself. 'Bring me at once,' says he, 'a hauberk and a helmet from Pavia, if you can put your hands on one.' – 'Yes,' they say, 'we have plenty.' They then unlocked a chest and took out a mail hauberk and a burnished helmet. All this they placed in front of him. He donned the bright hauberk, then laced the helmet on over it. His shield is brought to him along with the sword with the gilded baldric, which he hangs at his left side. The two maidens fitted a pair of spurs to his feet. Then he goes straight to the cellar where he had left the horse, and put on it a bridle and saddle. The horse gave no sign or indication at all that he had saddled it. Fergus sees it with great pleasure, aware that he now has a swifter and more valuable mount than the one he lost the previous day. He leaps energetically onto its back and puts it through its paces round the great hall. He then takes an enamelled lance they had brought him and which was keen and well honed.

4840   Out through the gate rode Fergus, descending the rock and digging in his steel spurs – if only he had already hurled himself among the besiegers and engaged with them! Gripped in his fists he held his lance. He clearly heard the bugles sounding the advance where they are opening the assault. Very plainly he heard the clamour of those manning the catapults; and they had already placed the ladders against the wall, evidently confident of taking the castle that day and seizing by force the lady who had held out against them for so long. Fergus, who has no single knight with him, feels great anger in his heart: he intends to go to prove himself quite alone, armed on his steed and under the eyes of the one who holds his heart. Ah, God! If only she knew that her lover was so close at hand: how glad and joyful she would be now! But before that she will be very grief-stricken.

4865   Fergus swoops down onto the camp, striking, shattering and toppling all he finds in his way. Before any of the attackers see him or anyone has noticed him, he has felled and slain four of their best nobles guarding the pavilions. To those carrying out the assault came a report that a knight had attacked the men left behind in the tents and that they were dying a tragic and shameful death. On hearing this news, the king at once calls his seneschal and has it proclaimed aloud everywhere that they

should immediately abandon the assault; and this they did without delay. If only you had seen them returning straight to the
shelters and tents, where the fight was to the death! When those
in the town see the attack being abandoned, they come straight
out with the biggest force of men they can muster, wishing to
engage those who form the rearguard.

4892   Fergus sees and observes all this, then thrusts himself back
into the thick of things. He brandishes, then lowers his good
lance: whoever he strikes a full blow with it will never be spared
death. The men of the army are very alarmed to see how he
destroys and confounds them all. They have far greater fear of
him whom they could see quite alone than of the others who
were pursuing them. The men from the town with their company
go provoking them from the rear; and in front Fergus leaps at
them, striking them with his sharp sword, anyone caught by its
blade being cloven right down to the saddle. The fight is fierce
and general. Fergus is seated on a very fine horse and goes franti-
cally seeking the king who was maintaining this siege. To his
sorrow, he could not find him. In his rage and anger he secured a
very good exchange: on his way he encountered the seneschal, a
man of high standing; so he struck him on his gemmed helmet
with the good sword that used to be Perceval's. He slices through
him down to the horse, pulls out his sword, and drops him dead.
Then those on his side are plunged in deep sorrow and say that
all is lost now the seneschal is vanquished.

4925   Fergus, however, does not pause at all. He renews his attack on
them like a lion, shouting to those from the castle: 'Strike now!
Those traitors and tricksters are done for. It was unlucky for
them that they came to besiege the lady!' Those from the castle
are overjoyed to hear him calling them on, and they strike with
lance and sword. Many a saddle was emptied and many a knight
defeated and slain. Stray chargers go galloping over the field
trailing their reins. But Fergus continues to encourage those from
up in the castle, urging them on, by word and deed, to be worthy
and valiant, proud and courageous in the fight. They follow

admirably; but the opposition is too strong for them, as they are outnumbered twenty to one. The losses on both sides are heavy.

4947 The maiden had climbed up on the tower to see the battle between her men and the king's. Her heart beats fast with great apprehension, since she fears and dreads that all the company will be slain. For she was quite unaware of the aid her lover had lent her, except that she does see the radiance that brightens up the day, though without knowing what that might be. She is very content to gaze at that sight, on which she fixes her whole attention, saying it is some supernatural creature come to her assistance. So she believes, and with good reason, whilst all say the same, high and low.

4964 No one dared to approach Fergus: on the contrary, they flee in panic like cowardly sheep. Those from the castle strive to their utmost, felling and killing many of their adversaries, and making a very hard battle of it. Fergus sees a man-at-arms approaching carrying an ashen lance. He addresses him very politely with the words: 'My friend, please give me that lance you're holding: that would be very kind and courteous of you.' The soldier does not refuse him, but hands it over, and Fergus takes it. Then he spotted in the jousting a knight, the king's nephew, who was treating very severely the defending knights there to their grievous damage, torment and anguish. He had killed so many that the steel sword in his grasp was covered in blood. Fergus thereupon rode up to him and shouted: 'Sir vassal, turn this way! You're behaving too badly in creating such havoc among those people. For I'm quite convinced that when this castle is taken, you won't be in charge of it!' The man turns quickly. Here now comes Fergus at the gallop! He strikes him with the ashen lance, knocking him clean over backwards. He thrusts hard at him, sending him to the ground; and then by the rein he takes the horse, which was worth fully a hundred silver marks. He hands it by the bridle to the youth who had given him the lance, saying: 'Young man, I find a lady I see up there very attractive. Lead this charger to her now on my behalf with a greeting. Then tell her that the Knight of the Shining Shield sends her this long-maned chestnut, having knocked a most distinguished knight off its back for her sake.'

5011   With that the fighting breaks up. Fergus leaves by a clearing in the forest made by the besiegers. They did not know where he had gone: they lost him straight away. Then those from the castle return there. The messenger does not idle his time away, but comes swiftly by a secluded path straight to the keep. Leading the charger with his right hand, he makes directly for the maiden. He holds the horse by the reins and, having first greeted her, he hands the steed over to her, saying it is sent her by the man who has carried off all the distinction and glory at the jousting: 'And you may be absolutely certain that he briskly unhorsed the king's nephew for love of you.' The daylight fades and the sun sets. The maiden went inside the castle and then asked the squire which way the knight who sent her the horse went. He could tell her nothing other than that he saw him enter the woods; but after that he did not know what became of him. The lady found what the young man told her most astonishing.

5042   Fergus rode and journeyed on until he arrived at the place where he was staying. The ladies had not ceased to lament since he left, for they believed he would certainly be slain there or captured through some mischance. When they see him they are jubilant. They lower the bridge at his approach and receive him happily. Fergus goes upstairs and disarms on the paved floor of the main hall. The two ladies had lit a great fire of hornbeam wood. The gallant, illustrious Fergus sat down on a couch side by side with the maidens, who asked him about the siege. And he told them everything about how he had acquitted himself and how the horse had been sent to the object of his love and desire. He never omitted to tell them anything he was able to recollect. Afterwards he asks for supper, having gone for a long time without eating. They leapt to it faster than the wind and brought it to him promptly, since it was ready prepared. You will not hear the courses described by me; but when they had eaten their fill, just

as much as they wished, his bed was made up, and he retired to
sleep, the maidens doing likewise.

5076   The next day at the crack of dawn he rises, takes the fine
splendid equipment of his, and goes back to fight at the siege.
Immediately they see him, the people of the town emerge, form-
ing their ranks in very orderly fashion and attacking from the
other side. In this way hostilities are reopened every day of the
week. Fergus gives the besiegers a hard time, handing out a very
harsh recompense for the ravages and hardships they had inflicted
on the lady. Should this affair last much longer the king is in a
grave plight unless he takes another course of action and either
makes a pact or turns to flight. He sees plainly that he could not
prevail against that supernatural knight. He has found him far
too much to manage, being afraid to approach him.

5098   To seek advice the king has all his vassals summoned. Then
they take to considering what he shall do about this matter. None
of them dares offer advice, for they all know for sure that to flee
would be too base, and if they stay they are all dead men and
neither the weak nor the strong will get away. Thus many of
them are in a quandary. A large number, the majority, say they
will never take to flight or make off out of fear. Most agree to
this. The king had a nephew, his sister's son, who was a courageous knight. That was the man whom Fergus toppled with the
ashen lance. Now hear what his proposal was. He rose to his feet
and said so that all heard him: 'Dear good uncle, now listen to
me. I see all your men more scared of one single knight than they
should be of a thousand. Why have them killed? Send in there, by
someone or other, a message to the maiden and townsfolk saying
they are holding against your will what belonged to your ances-
tors. Let them return it to us with proper affection. And assure
them further that you will let them all go with the exception of
the lady, who will remain with you for you to do with her as you
please. If it suits you, take her yourself; and if you're not happy
with her, then she'll be handed over to your serving-lads to have
in their power. And if anyone should contest your rightful claim

to Lothian, here is my immediate pledge to demonstrate here and now that this should be your fief.'

5143   They all backed that advice and unanimously advised the king that this is how the battle should be ended, if the maiden is prepared for her part to make an agreement along these lines. In order to reassure them and comply with their wishes, the king agreed to all this with them; for they really believed that there was no better warrior in the world than his nephew Arthofilaus. He said that he himself would go to her to make good his pledge, should anyone dare to stand up against him to contest it.

5158   With that he leaves the encampment and goes spurring off at a frantic pace all the way to Roxburgh and an entrance to the northwest. The guard at that postern gate immediately comes down; and Arthofilaus shouts roughly to the man: 'Open the gate, you scoundrel! It was devils made a porter out of you. Hurry and open up to me at once!' – 'By my faith, sir,' says the porter, 'just you make haste gently! First of all, I think, you'll tell me who you are and what you're after: otherwise you'll never set foot inside here.' – 'I'll tell you, son of a whore, and may God send you a bad day tomorrow! Is it then your lady's practice to have a message for her delivered at the gate? Really! Is she a shepherdess? By the faith I owe Saint Peter himself, I now have a lower opinion of her than I did when I set out on this journey!' Seeing and gathering that he has come as a messenger, the porter unlocks the gate.

5184   Arthofilaus, his lance raised, goes spurring through the street without greeting any man or woman. Then he dismounted at the block, leaving his lance and shield, and hitching his good, spirited steed to the olive tree. Up the steps goes Arthofilaus, the very image of a marquis or count. He hastens through the hall to where the lady was sitting privately with her household. Without so much as a greeting, he addresses her. 'My lady,' he says, 'just keep quiet! The king himself sends me to you, instructing you to wait no longer, but to surrender this town to him and place yourself at his mercy. He has arranged and stipulated just what he will do with you: he'll hand you over to his serving-lads, for he would no more deign to take you himself than jump into a bog! And if you're not prepared to abandon to him what is his to hold by right, then get someone to defend it for you! I'm prepared to be killed or hanged if I'm not ready to make good my pledge, should any of your men get to his feet!'

5213 The maiden was furious that he had insulted her like an uncouth fool, and said: 'Vassal, you've eaten or drunk on an empty stomach. I fancy you're one of Wasselin's three messengers.* A curse on whoever gave you the wine that's made you so drunk! Aren't you used to wine being so cheap, then? Indeed, it was very wrong of that king who sent you here not to have let you sleep instead. Go and rest a little; and then you'll be good enough to come back to spin us some of your yarns! How is your lord? I think he's been able to tell for some time how many bolts there are in the gates of this residence. He has plenty of opportunity to know, and count them if he wishes, to while away his time. I gladly give him my leave to think about it, and to go back when he wants to. He has no need to stop on my account.'

5239 Arthofilaus hears the insults addressed to him by the lady, and they annoy and hurt him very much: he almost bursts with shame. But he showed no sign of it, and replied to the lady: 'Maiden, I'm not at all surprised. You're a woman, so you speak nonsense. And it's no wonder to me that you've replied without reflection. Whoever you may be, you're a woman. But I tell you straight to leave this fief, which belongs to my lord. Otherwise I advise you definitely to look for a man with the courage to object to my lord having it. If you have anyone, here I am ready – or two against two if you prefer – should you have any hope for it.'

5258 Replying hastily, the lady uttered a rash boast. For, with extreme folly and in an amazing fit of temper, she said he should grant a week's respite, by the end of which she would find a knight who would fight, entirely on his own, the two best ones outside: he would be quite alone.* For neither he nor the king had any right to Lothian, to which he was laying claim. If he is agreeable, then let him go away on these conditions. The combat will be fought on the understanding that the two best men from the besiegers outside will arm themselves, and against them there will be a single man to defend the maiden. Arthofilaus hears the proposal; and in that way the combat is fixed and the arrangement for it concluded. He gave his solemn agreement to it; and the maiden swore to it for her part: if her man is vanquished, she will give up Lothian and submit forthwith and quite properly to the king's pleasure. And if by chance the two warriors happen to be defeated and vanquished in the combat, the king will return to his land without pursuing the war any further. Arthofilaus agrees to that, after which he makes his way back, and tells the king the substance of their negotiations. The king said: 'The person who has arranged such a combat against me has a low opinion of me, by Saint Richier! May God never come to my aid if, given the opportunity, I don't make her pay for it! Never in all my experience do I recall such an affront as she has subjected me to in her arrogance.' Thus the king discusses the matter and turns it over in his mind.

5302   In the castle, however, the damsel remains much preoccupied with her thoughts. She is very worried and full of regret that in her senseless folly she has committed herself to this duel. But her realisation has come too late, for the affair is so widely known that there is no concealing it. In her perplexity the maiden asks her knights to advise her whether there is anyone who for money or in defence of her territory would dare to undertake this combat. They all remain speechless and silent (devil a one makes a move!) except for a single man, a despicable fellow, who said: 'My lady, what business of ours are your misguided promises, if you made them? You took no advice about it from us. Attend to it yourself, if you want to: you've made the brew, so you drink it! You'll never get any help from us. Common sense is far better than recklessness;* but that's not at all how you've acted. You've started an affair that will turn out to your shame. A curse on anybody who feels sorry for you if you get nothing but trouble

from it!' The lady keeps her head bowed, because she knows well
and can see that she would find no help in the matter.

5333   She went weeping and quite despondent into her own room.
The maidens attending her approached her very respectfully,
telling her not to be dismayed, for the Lord God will help her.
*One of them, a very courtly and beautiful girl called Arondele,
said to her: 'Don't worry, but trust firmly in God. In my opinion,
though, if anyone could have news of that knight who has
emptied so many saddles and upended so many fighters on that
meadow for love of you, I believe he would come to your aid.
And if you are willing to give me leave without further delay,
then before noon has struck I'll go out secretly and quite alone
on my ambling mule. I'll not give up at all until I've found him.
But should I not find him, I'll go directly to the court of King
Arthur, who has so often come to the rescue of an orphaned lady
in distress. I'm certain his help won't be refused. Without a lie,
I'll bring you one of the company of the Round Table, if there's
one to be found at court. But I've no reason to delay any longer,
if you wish me to go: the combat's a week from today.'

5367   The maiden is extremely pensive and would rather be dead
than alive. Nevertheless, she was cheered a little by Arondele
asking her permission to go on the quest, if she was willing. But
she must take very good care not to be away more than a week. 'I
won't,' she said. She takes her leave and then makes straight for
a hidden stable. With her mule very well harnessed, she mounts
and sets out quite alone, without company.

5381   She rode and journeyed until, at the end of three days, she
found the king in Carlisle, where he was staying. But he was very
sad and dejected because he had none of his company with him:
he had sent them all away in search of a knight he had lost and
whom he had heard called Fergus. He had not seen him since he
had dubbed him and he had set off to seek the horn. So the king
was very alarmed. My lord Gawain had headed straight across a
heath, and Perceval was in Pelande; Sir Kay the seneschal was
elsewhere, in Galloway; Sir Sagremor the Impetuous had gone to

Saragossa; Erec was riding through Scotland; and Lancelot had gone to Wales. So they had all dispersed; and it had already been a month and a half since they had set out on that quest. When they left, they had agreed among themselves all to return together on the day they would fix. It was, as we know for a fact, precisely on Ascension Day that they were to return if they found the knight, and equally so if he was not found.*

5412   The maiden's spirits completely sank. Seeing that she would find none of those on whom she was pinning great hope, she no longer knows where to place her trust. So she laments: 'Alas, wretch that I am! My lady has placed such false reliance on me! I've betrayed her! She's relying on me to find help. Alas! I really did intend to help her; but I'll never give her any assistance!' Hearing her lamenting so, the king said, in order to cheer her up: 'My fair one, don't grieve so! I firmly believe that they'll be back within twelve days; and then I'm sure they will help you.' – 'That day and time's no use to me,' says the girl. 'But tell me where I would find my lord Gawain, if I went to look for him.' – 'He went to Galway,* my sweet. But if you go that way, you might soon come to some place where you could hear news of him.' She takes her leave and parts from the king. She rides straight in the direction where she thinks she may find Gawain. Her efforts, though, are in vain, since she will not find him. She passes through the whole of Galway without being given any guidance, and there were no more than two full days left before the time-limit. Like it or not, the maiden has to return in despair, not having been able to discover anything at all that she had been seeking.

5452   On Sunday, just about noon, the damsel passes through Melrose, where the fortified tower built by the giant was situated. As she goes past it, she finds that devil lying on a hillside, and stops for some time. Fergus was amusing himself on top of the tower and, looking towards the slope, saw the maiden in a secluded spot gazing at the giant lying on the ground. So he goes to ask her where she has come from and where she is bound. Having gone down from the tower, he takes her by the bridle and greets her. Despite being quite taken aback, she returns his greeting very politely and courteously. Fergus said to her: 'My sweet friend, where are you from? Don't conceal it from me, by the faith you owe me.' – 'Sir, I'll not disguise the fact from you that I was born in this country; and yet, I assure you, I've never known before in all my life that there was any castellan's residence here. It's a very handsome fortress.' Fergus replies: 'My damsel, it's only right that you should know. Come in and shelter here; and you'll have excellent hospitality, because the castle's in my keeping. It's very proper that you should have lodging here.'

5486 – 'Thank you, sir,' says the maiden. 'I'm most grateful to you; but I'll not accept. I can still very well get to Roxburgh tonight, by the time it grows dark. I'll have small comfort for my lady when I reach her. I've utterly failed to keep the promise I'd made her – of that I'm only too well aware! Why should I hide it? When she knows for sure that she'll not have any help for the combat that's been agreed on oath, she will kill herself on the spot!' – 'She certainly won't, my very sweet sister: God wouldn't on any account allow your lady to take her own life in this way! Didn't she, then, ever have as a lover any knight who would undertake this task?' – 'No, sir, so help me God! No man ever had a relationship with her, and she never loved any knight save one (and he soon walked out on her), with whom she fell in love at Liddel. His name was Fergus. She found him very attractive, as I've heard her tell. But he didn't want to be her lover before he'd successfully fought a combat he had undertaken. My lady was so distressed at this that she couldn't stay there. Instead she left, without the knowledge of her uncle, who was grief-stricken. Since then she's never heard of the knight I'm speaking of and doesn't know if he's dead or alive. But it seems to me she still loves him. She'll not last long, though, because I'm convinced she will kill herself before she's prepared to agree to this king marrying her.'

5527 Fergus hears this and is delighted. He said: 'My sweet, kind friend, by the faith I owe you you shall stay with me tonight.

Then, if you wish, I'll put you on the road early in the morning. And you may be sure and confident that, if that man has heard of his beloved's plight, he will be false if he does not go to her aid. As for me, I swear to you that, if she loved me like that, I'd give her real assistance, and just as soon as I could. But tell me this: how long ago that king laid siege to her like this and whether she's had any help since.' – 'No, sir, except that for seven days last week an armed knight came out of this great leafy forest to give the king and his men a rough and humiliating time. The combat, and I'm not wanting to lie to you, was arranged out of faith in him. I've sought him for a long time, but can't find him. I'd be confident that, if I did find him, I should beg him in love's name until he rescued my lady, however busy he was. But why should I look for him any more? I'd wear myself out to no purpose, because the unequal combat of one knight against two is due to be held tomorrow. Alas! The odds are quite unfair!' Such are the girl's words.

5564   Fergus hugs and embraces her, saying: 'Dismount, my friend, because, upon my word, you'll not go any further tonight, if you want to please me. You shall take your lodging straight away up there in that castle: I'll be all the better for your company.' The maiden replies: 'That's impossible. For I pledged my lady with my right hand when I left her that I'd come back this evening. So I must go on. But if you wouldn't object or think I was just prattling – in God's name, who killed this devil?' – 'My lady,' said he, 'I suppose the man with the blazing shield who came to your lady's aid vanquished him with his naked sword. For I know that and saw it clearly: I wasn't very far from here. Then he spent the night in this castle, went the next day to the siege, and against the king inflicted great damage on the very pick of his nobility. And if you had that man, you could have every confidence that he'd not fear, without a word of a lie, to take on two knights. But I want you to know this: he doesn't live in this castle, and yet he'll be staying here before three days have passed. But the deadline's very close, when you say it will be

tomorrow.' She replies: 'That's true. It can't be postponed: that
is how it was sworn and pledged by both parties. But now give
me my leave. I've stayed too long I think.'

5605   When Fergus hears that there is nothing he can do to make
her stay, he reluctantly gives her her leave. He leads her to the far
edge of the forest, continually comforting her. Then he said
that, if God Almighty pleases, the knight will return and defend
the maiden. With that they did not converse any longer, but
parted. He goes away; and the girl continues on, grieving, until
she comes to Roxburgh. She found the lady in the middle of the
hall, quite pale from weeping since she never stopped, day or
night. All her joy, pleasure and beauty have been washed away;
and she would not have recovered them, however she might
prosper, in one of the longest summer days. Seeing the girl
approaching, she went and seized her by the cloak, which was of
fine white woollen material. She asks her for her news. But none
she told her gave her any pleasure or satisfaction or any cause
for hope. Her great grief and misery cause her to fall to the
ground on her back in a swoon.

5634   Her nobles having raised her up, each of them sternly
reproaches her for swooning so often. They say she will not be
too debased when this king has married her after she fails to get
help. 'Be quiet, you stinking slanderers!' says the maiden angrily.
'May Jesus Christ bring bad luck and torment on you! You're so
good at comforting me! You go off to him if you want to, because
you'll certainly never get a taste of the wedding between him and
me: there's no need to get worked up about that!' With that she
goes into her room, and her maidens go in after her. They calmed
her down and looked after her attentively. Otherwise she would
have done away with herself. They watched over her closely until
evening and then put her to bed, thinking she would quieten
down and rest a little. But she turned her thoughts elsewhere.

5658   All night long she weeps and wails, saying: 'Alas, miserable as
I am! How unlucky for me I was ever born! I'm utterly wretched,
and rightly so. God, why am I hesitating before plunging a knife

straight into my breast?* Am I then waiting for that wicked, criminal king to get me in his clutches? May evil fevers grip him and hellfire burn him before he ever has me in his keeping! In his keeping? May it not please God that I ever perform his service! That would be shameful for my lover. – Lover? Alas, what am I saying? It was very presumptuous of me to say that. Would I, then, force my love on him? How, then, do I know whether he's dead or alive? I don't believe he's dead, by Saint Denis: I'd have plainly noticed that. The bright sun would have lost a third of its beauty, had my lover lost his life.

5681   'It's been fully two years since I've seen him. It wasn't through anything at all blameworthy on his part; but it's I who should be done away with for not at least waiting for him to return to Liddel. My uncle would have given him to me, had I asked him, because he was so extremely handsome. Handsome? – Yes, certainly: even far too much so! His face's colouring is such that it might have been painted, to the extent that, if he chose to wash his face in a river or the clear sea and anyone washed after him, he too was quite coloured. The truth is plain to see: my dear, sweet love, how great is my loss, for I shall not have you in this hour of need and know that I'll never see you again. Tomorrow before the hour of prime I shall throw myself off my tower, and that moment will see the end of me!'

5704   All night long until morning the maiden lamented, without ever drinking or eating or being able to rest. The next day when it was about to grow light, she gets up and goes to church to hear mass and the service. Once it has been spoken and sung, the maiden left and went away with her household, depressed, grieving and sorrowful. Again she reveals her thoughts to them, saying that she will freely hand over herself and all her treasures to the man who will take up arms to go out to the combat. Let her go and look elsewhere for someone to go, for among them all there is not a single one who ever laces on his helmet!

5723   The king was the first to arrive at the tower; and with him rides his nephew, dashing along on his charger. At the top of his voice he shouts to them: 'Lady, are you sleeping in this morning? Have you forgotten the combat? Here I am all ready and ask for nothing else. What does it mean that no man's coming forward with the heart to fight both of us? Let him step forward quickly! Is this some trick, then? Otherwise, empty this town for me! By Saint Paul, there will be a heavy price to pay for having put it off for so long! I think the dues earned from me by those wicked traitors will be settled, though!'

5740   The lady had gone without companions to the highest turret in her whole keep. She had gone there alone because she does not enjoy or appreciate being comforted by anyone, and so as to throw herself off from there in order to end her life. She goes to stand by a pillar some hundred and eighty feet above the ground. From there she measures her leap. She gathers her clothes tightly about her, quite determined that they should not be caught by the wind and her fall impeded. The maiden commends herself to God, not asking for anything other than to put an end to her life. She is in such anguish that she calls out: 'Fergus, my sweet love, my life has run its course! This very day you will lose your true love: she will never be rescued by you. You wait and delay too long. You'll never set eyes on me again, for today will see my parting from you: make no mistake about that! I commend you to God the Father.'

5768   Having said that, she steps forward, makes the sign of the cross on her face with her right hand, then puts her head at the window to let herself slip down. But God is unwilling to suffer the loss of a soul there: she hears at that moment a voice saying to her: 'Maiden, you are not at all wise: look over towards the woods!' That much it said, then fell silent. The maiden looked at them and saw the forest lit as brightly as if it were on fire.* The more she looked, the brighter it was made by the one bringing the radiance. And if anyone should take issue with me as to why the maiden was so startled by that shield, having seen it just as bright and shining on another occasion, I shall show him briefly that she had never before seen it endowed with the same beauty as then. It is an established fact that on that morning there had been a slight dew, and the shield was a trifle damp with it. The sun then shoots its beams straight onto the paintwork, which shines with a blazing light, one of the shield's constant properties being that when it was moistened, it shone much more brightly and was far more beautiful and attractive.*

5802   The king, waiting for the combat, had climbed onto a lookout point, where he could never be on the alert for anyone attacking him unless he came from the town, towards which he was facing. Here now comes Fergus at a furious gallop, shield on arm! You will soon see justice upheld without any solemn pledge or formal rebuttal; no oath will be taken or any other condition laid down! Fergus, afire with prowess, called wrathfully to the two men: 'You are spies, I believe. By the faith I owe you, I'd very strongly recommend you to go on your way, if you're prepared to take my advice!' The king promptly replies: 'Sir, what's this to do with you? I have a combat to fight here and now, my nephew and I, against a knight who should come armed out of that town: it's to obtain my right and my heritage, which this lady is wrongly occupying. I really wonder why he's not coming.'

5831   Fergus replies to the king: 'By God, you don't appear to me very confident, when you've brought company along. By my faith, you're not just a little afraid of that lady in there! Are these your conditions, now? Is this your way of fixing combats: two knights against one? This isn't at all a good arrangement. Are you and your companion twin children, then? In the old days they used to stipulate that a pair of twins would fight against one man, if they were summoned. This practice has lapsed;* so it's a great shame and a pity when a combat of that kind is considered. Go back to your own district and take your people away with you, for you have nothing to do with this land, and ought not to lay claim to it. Hurry off before you have an unfortunate experience here!'

5854   Arthofilaus sweats with rage and would have burst with wrath, had he not deflated a little. In his fury he said something

it would have been far better for him to have left unspoken.
Arthofilaus was very arrogant and will now show his true face.
He said to Fergus: 'Sir rogue, why should we flee from here? Will
it be for fear of you? Do you think we're so timid? A curse on
anybody who believed that and who made that arrangement! If
it was you, then a curse on you! You've really terrified us now! By
the faith I owe Saint Peter the Apostle, he will have everything
despite you: the land and the whole fief; and he'll have the lady as
his wife.' Fergus was not amused by that: on the contrary, he put
him firmly in his place before he parted from him. But first he
spoke a few courtly, sensible words to him, saying: 'You're full of
scorn, by the faith I owe Saint Nicholas! But I'm not worried if a
knave voices his knavery. I hereby challenge you for my beloved:
for both the fief and the lady together. It seems to me I can see
her there. I want to play the lover's part for her sake. Stand back
now! I challenge you!'

5887   That is the end of the talking. The two men go off in one direction; and Sir Fergus out of courtesy made his circuit below the
tower, wanting to be seen there by that lady whose eyes are tear-
filled in her head. They have made their circuits, and now they
charge, holding their lances levelled. Fergus brandishes his own
lance, and the two opponents, riding close beside each other, both
strike him on his shield; but they did not rock or stagger him any
more than if he had been a castle. And Fergus strikes Arthofilaus
with his lance with its greenish tip. He splits and shatters his
heart. He showed very great strength: he felled the knight dead
and without his soul – a calamity for him, since it took leave of
his body. Fergus spurs on past, leaving him bleeding. When he
turned and came back, he gibed at him: 'You take this payment on
my sweetheart's account! If you'd had the sense to understand, a
good flight's better than a bad wait! Whoever may have the lordship of that castle, it will be a long time before you have possession
of it! I give you leave to have a long sleep-in in this meadow: you
got up too early this morning and didn't sleep well last night.
Now we'll go to do business with that other standard-bearer!'

5921   Fergus spurs towards the marble tower to comfort the girl whom he well knew to have suffered great anguish. Now, if he had his way, he would like to hold her on his charger's neck. He would kiss her, I fancy, more than a hundred times at one go. The king is not free of sadness. When he sees his nephew is dead, no living creature gives him pleasure or enjoyment. He went over to him at once, wishing to carry him away in his arms, while he sees Fergus amusing himself at the bottom of the meadow. Fergus spies him and calls out to him: 'By God, sir king, you'll leave him there! I've put him in charge of the fields and made him guardian of them and their crops. You yourself will find it very hard to save your skin before you get away from me.' With that he launched an attack on him, and dealt him a great blow high up. The king was full of wickedness, and Fergus did not spare him at all, but struck him, splitting his shield. He rends and rips his hauberk and drives his lance-head against his side, but without touching the flesh. He does however knock him, at the full length of his lance, onto the hard ground. Then he comes up to him with drawn sword.

5954   The king is in very deep distress. It is clear to him that there is no question of his getting up. If he is not prepared to call for mercy, he will quickly have his head taken off. Anyone lying like this at the feet of his mortal enemy would be only too glad to plead for mercy. I am not surprised, I swear, that this is what happens with the king when he saw Death approaching to attack and harass him. One should not be too critical of him, since he could evade Death only by calling for mercy. I would gladly do as much and beg to be spared death! The king has fallen into the net from which he will not emerge without demeaning himself. Be that as it may, he does utterly humble himself and call to Fergus for mercy, saying he is no longer able to resist or defend himself against him. Now he can kill or hang him, as he is vanquished and overcome and has no force, power, valour or might to withstand him. Faced with the king's insistent and urgent pleas for mercy, Fergus has no inclination or wish to do him any harm.

5984   In a generous, noble-hearted manner he speaks to him: 'Sir king, you are well aware that it's up to me whether I kill or pardon you. But if you're prepared to go to the court of my lord the king accoutred and equipped as you are at present, I'll forgive you on this occasion for the anger and annoyance you've caused me. Understand, though, that before you leave me I wish you to restore to the lady, peaceably and in total freedom, her castles and fortresses, her men you have captured and her friends whom you have wrongfully conquered. If you decline to do this, then by Him who lights the world, all the gold on earth will not save you from dying at once by my sword!'

6005   Now when the king hears and sees that there would be no other escape for him, he grants his wishes as he had expressed them and will do all in his power to fulfil them: before the evening has passed he will return to the lady everything she can claim against him; and then he will go straight to that court which is the source of high renown. Fergus makes him pledge as much and has him declare he would do just what he had first told him. Afterwards he instructed him to say, on his arrival at court, that he had been overcome at arms by Fergus, a gallant, bold knight, whom Kay drove away by his talk. And he should tell the seneschal that on the very first occasion he has to catch him, he will give him such reward as he has deserved from him. All this he swore and pledged; and when the deal was concluded, Fergus makes one request of him: that he shall go by way of the castle and greet the maiden on behalf of the anonymous knight who could not have offended her more.

6035   Once the king had agreed to all this, the two of them parted, with the king staying there and Fergus going away. The maiden is sad and melancholy when she sees him making off without her being able to speak to him. Fergus enters the forest, whilst the maiden follows after him with her eyes but in no other way. The king waits no longer, but climbs onto a horse. Dejected, heavy-hearted and miserable, he first of all goes to the town to fulfil his agreement concerning the message to the queen.* With a gloomy expression and bowed head he rides on to Roxburgh. Passing right through the town, he comes directly to the square keep. The lady had come down from it and gone into a nearby church to pray to God. Having finished her prayers, she returned to her keep; and on her way she met the king. She was very upset by this encounter, since he had committed many serious offences against her, and will commit another before long: he is likely to tell her something that will bring her joy and grief, if it is possible on any score to feel both joy and grief. She will be joyful at one thing and then afterwards will be sad. Her joy will come from knowing for sure that the king will make no further claim on her inheritance: Fergus her lover has fully established her rights by his great valour. But, once she learns the truth, she will be most distressed not to have spoken to him.

6077　　The king, sweating with shame, sees and greets the lady. Then he said: 'Listen, maiden: I give you back all your inheritances and won't retain a single stronghold. But you'll be wrong to be grateful to me, because I'm very sorry to do it. If I'd had my way, you'd not have had them back like this for a very long time. I've been badly fooled and taken in by a knight (may God confound him!) than whom there's no better in the whole world. I don't know who he is (may God shame him!); but he did just tell me to say to you that he was a knight who, he fears, was responsible for angering you as never before. That much he said to me and then went away.' When the lady hears what he says, she reflects just for a moment and then says that this is the man who rejected her and her love. Then she firmly concludes that he was quite without hope of winning her love. Thereupon Love launches a fresh attack on her, and she goes away up to her great hall. But I do not wish now to go into her suffering and grief, such as Love is expert at inflicting.

6107　　The king has delivered his message and at the same time handed back everything he had taken from the lady. He goes away full of grief and wrath. Already the army was in uproar, having heard the news that their lord had been overcome and

Arthofilaus done to death. They all weep inconsolably and say:
'Death has found him, since he had no leave to live on!' Thereupon
they see the king coming; and they mock him bitterly for having
given poor protection to themselves and his nephew, whom they
had found so valiant. 'My lords,' says he, 'you're wrong in what
you say. I for my part am completely frustrated. The situation
was, I swear to you, that if ten of you were with me fully armed
on the field, may I never find favour with the Lord God if a single
one of you would have got away without your all being cut to
ribbons. Yet you'd have done him no injury at all, because he's as
hard as metal. A curse on the father who sired him, for he's done
us great harm by killing my nephew for me! Go back to your
country, because the siege has to be abandoned. We can't carry
the war on any longer, nor do I want to break my word.' Then
you might have seen that army disperse and the tents dismantled.
And the king has his nephew taken and carried away to his land.
That war is completely at an end. Each man goes away to his
own region. The king, without waiting any longer, goes directly
to Cumberland and asks the way to Carlisle.

6149   *He rode on his journey until a day of solemn celebration that
was very important and highly venerated. It was called Ascension
Day, one of the year's great festivals, as we are truthfully assured.
On that day he arrived armed exactly as he was on the day Fergus
vanquished him. It was in the summer month of May, when the
woodland bursts into leaf and the meadow grows green, and
each true lover sings new ditties and songs for his sweetheart.
With his nobles King Arthur was holding his full, munificent
court with a happy air and in good humour: never had he held a
richer one, for his company had returned having been on their
quest for a winter and that much of the summer. Mass had been
recited and sung. In the court they had sounded the horn for the
water and sat down at the tables. Then you would have seen the
stewards and attendants serving everywhere. King Arthur sat at
the end of a fixed beechwood table, holding a little stick which
he was whittling with a knife. He was deep in thought and sighed

continually. While they were eating, high and low, King Arthur's thoughts were so much on Fergus that he neither ate nor drank. My lord Gawain notices that his uncle is brooding, but he has no wish to speak to him about it.

6185   King Arthur remained in his reverie for a long time until he saw coming through the gate the man bringing that news which will be extremely welcome at court. He never drew rein until he came to the block beneath the olive-tree, where he tethers his horse. Then he mounts the stairs fully armed. Coming through the hall straight to the table where the king is seated, he greets him by name and all the nobility around him. Then he said: 'I give myself up as your prisoner. Though it grieves me, I cannot refuse to tell of my sorry situation, my grief and my woe.' Having no wish to lie to them, he tells them everything without waiting any longer: how he left his land and how the knight with the splendid shield attacked him at the siege, and how he defeated him in armed combat. He related everything to them, omitting nothing, and declared that there never was such a knight and never will be. 'His name is Fergus: that is how he named himself to me when he sent me here. After that, he told me I should place myself in your captivity, and that I should say this much to the seneschal: that it was unlucky for him that he mocked him; and he has not yet forgotten it.'

6219   Hearing what he said, the jester leaps up and begins to shout aloud: 'Sir Kay, don't be sad about that, for before long we'll see you fishing, and don't doubt it, head down out of courtesy!' When the seneschal heard the fool ridiculing him in this way, he felt nothing but rage. In his hand he held a knife with a blade two feet long. He angrily flung his weapon, hurling it at the jester. He does not hit him, much to his annoyance, and the jester takes to his heels. The king, when he saw that violent act, could not refrain from saying to him: 'My lord Kay, that was wrong of you! If you'd killed that little jester, what praise would it have earned you? It would have been held against you for all time. You're too quick-tempered. Through your vicious prattlings you've taken

from me that outstanding noble, which I don't think at all funny.
A curse on the tongue that can't resist this continual backbiting!'
So the king rebukes Kay for the arrogant, outrageous act he had
seen him commit against the jester. But his words were utterly
wasted, for they never caused Kay to hold back.

6250 King Arthur excused the captive king his imprisonment for
the love of the noble lord who had defeated him in combat; and
he retained him at court. They all shower him with praise and
affection. Those courtly folk give themselves over to much merry-
making and pleasure. But whoever may have rejoiced, the king
remained silent, for his heart was elsewhere. When they had risen
from their meal, those powerful knights went to sit in groups.
The king, my lord Gawain, the captive king and Yvain, just the
four of them together, had a discussion and conferred among
themselves; but the subject of their conversation was of nothing
but the merit and valour of Fergus and of his heroism. No man
of his age possessed so much. The king himself declared that he
would no longer hesitate to go in person to seek him through
forests and over sea and land, if my lord Gawain approves: there
is no land this side of the Danube where he would not go to look
and enquire for him, to see if he could find a trace of him.

6279 'By God,' says the captive king, 'you'll not be put to all that
trouble to seek him or get information! I saw him enter the forest
at Roxburgh, believe me; and if you take my advice you'll go that
way to look for him, if you are so very fond of him as you appear
to be. I'm sure you'll find him there, because he's often in that
forest.' The king replies: 'That suits me, if my nephew is prepared
to agree.' Gawain said: 'I don't want to turn that advice down;
but there's something more worth while, if anyone thought of
putting it to you. Travelling is a hard and wearisome business.
*But have a tournament proclaimed, quite seriously and not as a
joke, in the plains by Jedburgh and lasting a fortnight or a month.
Let the tournament be known about everywhere. And when it
breaks up, the prizewinner will be given a marriage to his taste
and will be crowned king of some realm, if he requests it: he must

be quite assured of that. If Fergus is in this country, he'll come to it, I promise you. In however distant a region he may be, when he hears all the talk and the proclamation of the tournament, he will go there straight away, if he has any love of chivalry.'

6314　King Arthur agrees to everything his nephew suggests to him. He at once sends out his summons everywhere, saying that no knight should refrain from coming promptly to take part in a tournament on the plain below Jedburgh which is to last more than a fortnight. Everywhere the report flies that all the very gallant nobles at King Arthur's court have arranged a fort-night's tournament. Everybody obeys the summons: no one hides or keeps out of sight, but they all turn up in the hope of gain. The tournament, I swear, took a whole month to assem-ble. The captive king wishes to leave, not feeling like taking part in it: instead, he was brooding sadly and dejectedly on the great loss he had suffered. As he did not wish to join in the entertainment, he asked his leave of King Arthur. The king has no mind to cross him, having excused him from his imprison-ment and declared him at liberty. So that king departs, and that is the end of that.

6340　The news spread until Galiene got to hear of the fact that King Arthur had nobly initiated that tourney. She called her lords before her to advise her, saying that she must take steps to make a good marriage, since from now on she cannot rule her land without a man's help. So they should give her their view, with her honour in mind, on whom she should take as a husband to defend herself and her land. She does not wish to take any without their advice. Now they do not know what to suggest to her except that it would be best for her to go to court to speak to the king who has assembled this tournment; and she should request and beg him to marry her as he pleased to a man with whom she would be well placed and not be marrying beneath her. That is the advice of great and small; and she was intent on nothing else but to be able to go to court. If they had each opposed her, she would still have gone despite them to speak to the emperor, and not so much to speak to him as to discover if she would see there the man with the splendid shield. That is the man she would ask the king for, because she gives herself entirely to him and on him she freely confers her love. She loves that man, and if she does not have him she will accept none of the others. The maiden meekly agreed to do just as they wished and never to go against their advice.* She made all the preparations for her journey.

6381   Time passed until the date for the tournament was fixed. And Fergus was well aware of it, having heard the talk of it which had spread everywhere. Report has it that one Tuesday before the feast of Saint John all the renowned knights from the land of England had assembled. They had come in pursuit of chivalry and to gain a name and reputation in order to pit themselves against those known as 'the test'. I refer to those of the Table, who act as a test for the whole world. What more should I tell? Both sides assembled. The king with all his company took up his position by Jedburgh. An amazing body of knights gathers opposite him. They proceed into the desolate forest and set up their lists with stout barriers that could be let down: it was a scene of lively activity.

6408   The night passes, and the day arrives. The knights take up their arms as if burning and eager to get to grips with each other. They are drawn up on both sides and come onto the field at once. My lord Kay, fully armed on a black horse, leaves the ranks, because already the previous evening he had asked for the opening joust.* The king reluctantly granted it to him because he was the first to request it. He takes the lead before them all in coming forward to joust, if he can find an opponent. Immediately, out of the woods there sprang Fergus on the light-coloured horse that runs faster than a small bird flies. When the men in the ranks spied him, they all stopped stock-still, saying: 'It's unfortunate the tournament was ever arranged and begun: it may well be that God has sent a flail to scourge us all. You'll soon see one man overthrown – and to his grief, whoever it is!

Who will be bold enough to face up to him without flinching?' –
'That will be Kay, the seneschal, who has just been pushing
himself forward.' – 'No it won't! He'd soon take to his heels if
he saw him approaching.'

6440   Fergus clearly hears them talking and is delighted and overjoyed that Kay, his mortal enemy, was to be the first to joust. If
he does not empty his stirrups for him, then he will have a very
low opinion of himself! He goes galloping hard to where he
sees Sir Kay spurring forward. He digs his spurs into his steed,
and Kay does likewise. Now Morial runs at Flori,* and they
clash at once. The joust was on some marshy ground beside a
flowing spring. Fergus strikes Kay plumb on the chest, knocking him and his northern horse down into a quagmire. Kay flies
backwards over the saddle into the stream running from the
spring, head-first like an acrobat, digging his flowered helmet
into the ground.

6461   Fergus sees him and bursts out laughing, saying: 'By my faith,
good sir, you're very bad-mannered to fish in my river without
my permission: you really have behaved outrageously! Now the
king can carry on with the tournament. He'll have plenty of fish
to eat this evening, if you can manage it! No man with such a
steward can be badly provided for. You've made an eel-trap with
your byrnie! It's a wonderful time you're having! I know you
didn't want the eel to get through the mesh. Keep a reckoning of
whatever you've caught, and don't let there be anything left
when you've finished! You're extremely greedy in your anxiety
to take everything; but you should leave at least some food, so
that when somebody else wants to fish he'll be able to find something.' My lord Kay cannot get up out of the mire into which he
has plunged. He would never have got out by himself had not
someone extricated him.

6488   With this joust behind him, Fergus turns away roaring with
laughter, then at once returns to where he sees the press at its
thickest. They all paid for the passes he made: there is nobody he
does not fell to the ground at once, provided he takes the trouble.

Lancelot goes riding between the ranks calling for a joust. Fergus
looks up and sees him coming. He has no intention or wish to
flee, but turns his charger towards him and, striking him on the
front of the shield, bears him to the ground. Then he sets spurs
to his horse and leaves him lying on the field. Wherever he goes
he really leaves his mark! Fergus strikes them all down like that,
being intent that day on nothing but toppling one upon the other.
In the end, with lance in rest, he plunged into the forest at a point
different from that where he arrived, because he wanted to
conceal himself so that no one would be able to find him.

6513   Fergus goes away to his retreat. King Arthur has his nobles
withdraw from the general engagement, and each of them goes
to his lodging. The others make for the forest, having taken an
amazing amount of booty; for they had secured all those felled
by Fergus, apart from Sir Kay and Lancelot, who received very
prompt and efficient help. That night there was no talk other
than of the one with the splendid shield. Gawain said he is
most valiant, but that he found it quite amazing that he never
showed any concern whatsoever for capturing a knight, but
only for unhorsing and toppling him. He had himself much
discussed that day, having given the knights a hard time. They
all think he is superhuman, because no knight he struck stayed
on his horse. King Arthur himself could not have praised him
more highly: all, great and small, are full of his praise, and even
Lancelot kept saying that he never before saw such blows struck.
But in no way was Kay able to praise or glorify him, in view of
the fact that he had sent him fishing: because of that he just
went on criticising him.

6544   The following day on the stroke of prime the distinguished
lords assemble. Sagremor asked the king for the favour of the
first joust in order to make the acquaintance of that noble man,
should he return to the fray. He proceeds to dash onto the field
and make his horse rear up. No one makes a move to joust against
him, because they were waiting for the one who had been there
the previous day and whom they expected to return. Fergus does

not keep them waiting, but extremely craftily emerges from the woods over by the town before launching himself back onto the plain. The joust between those two will soon be brought to a conclusion, whoever may regret it. With lances raised, each spurs and races at the other as hard as he can go. The king had moved forward a little to watch the joust. The two of them gallop on with lances braced and their shields on their arms. They deal each other mighty blows; but there is no more comparison between them than between a gerfalcon and a diver, for Fergus was ten times as agile, light and nimble as was Sagremor. He strikes him a blow with the lance in his fist full on the boss of his shield; and there is no girth, breast-strap, saddle-bow or the saddle itself that does not break. He sends him flying, legs in air, over his steed's crupper.

6580   Then the general engagement of the knights is resumed on the field. You might have seen there many a pennon, one man falling, another fleeing, one jousting, another yielding. There is a general exchange of blows. The king's side suffers many losses. Fergus is always in the thick of things without pause or halt, and nobody dares to wait and face up to him. Then here comes Perceval, who gave Fergus the sword. At once the cry goes up that this is Perceval the Welshman, than whom the king has no finer noble, other than the gallant Gawain.* The shouting increases on all sides. Fergus clearly catches sight of him and is in no doubt from what he hears and sees that this is the man who presented him with the sword. For that reason, not wanting to put him to shame, he evaded him for a while, turning his face in another direction and pretending not to see him. Then Perceval hails him in a loud voice: 'Turn this way, noble knight! You'll have to let me know who you are, if you please: I think you will tell me your name before we part.'

6610   When Fergus hears these words, he is very ashamed and annoyed. He would never seek to joust with him, since he had done him great honour; yet if he turned back, everyone would certainly be convinced that he had done so out of fear; and therefore he does not want to turn away from him. Instead, he goes to deal him a heavy blow at full lance's length, causing him to spring backwards, like it or not. He did nothing more, but went away again without stopping at all. Approaching in full view he sees the Black Knight whom he sent to serve at court; and as soon as he spotted him, he very easily recognised him and struck him violently on the shield, knocking him down onto the sandy ground. To rescue him there was a great clashing of arms and the din of swordstrokes. Fergus, however, does not linger, but goes secretly into the great, extensive forest. With that the king departs with his company, and those on the other side go away to their quarters. For the whole of that week Fergus comes to the tournament in the very same way. All praise him with one accord and declare that he is the complete victor: he has the praise and esteem of everybody.

6645   One Friday, I understand, a little before evening, the exquisite Galiene arrived at court in high spirits to request the king, in courtly and prudent fashion, to arrange her marriage. The maiden was not foolish: she herself put her whole case to the king in her own words, saying: 'By the Holy Spirit, good king, don't be disdainful if I tell my story myself. I am the lady of Lothian. A full year ago today my father unfortunately died. The inheritance has passed to me, and I assure you there's no heir to it except myself. A king has laid waste all my estates and fiefs, as you are very well aware. Over forty days ago I sent you my maiden to seek aid and assistance; but she did not find at court any of the men she was seeking.* A gallant, courtly knight came to my rescue, for which I thank him. I don't know who he is and have never seen him since. He brought my war to a happy conclusion for me. Now I have come to put to you, as I should to my lord, the request that you take care of me so that I don't become disinherited. A land left to a woman is badly governed. It should not displease you if from now on I should wish to improve my situation. It is high time for me to marry; but you may be sure I would take no man unless I had him from your court. When you give him to me, then I'll have him: otherwise I shall never accept anyone.'

6683   The king replies: 'My sweet friend, by the faith I owe Holy Mary, I will give you someone just as you please, since I should very much like to see your advantage and your honour, so help me God, if I could achieve them. Look throughout my realm: there will be no noble so distinguished there that, if you care to ask for him, I am not prepared to give him to you.' – 'By Saint Matthew, sire,' she says, 'I can tell you that I've not seen today that man I wish to ask you for. Never have I set my eyes on anyone more handsome than he. If I had looked carefully all day long, I should ask for no one, whatever his power or strength, but him of the splendid shield. Give me that man, if you have no objection. He pleases me: he's the one for me.' The king said: 'My dear friend, I have no idea who that is you are asking for, nor where he is nor where he was born, unless it is the man who every day arrives so early at this jousting bearing a blazing shield that shines as brightly as the sun and who is mounted on a greyish horse.' – 'Yes, sir, so help me God! That's the man, without a doubt. Give him to me, if you please; because it is he I truly love.' The king replied: 'How could I give him to you, when he's not willing to stay and speak with any man or make himself known? He's too reserved and proud, in my eyes.'

6721   The king called over my lord Gawain, his intimate, to advise him; and he came at once. Then the king tells him briefly what the maiden is requesting; and afterwards he asks his opinion on how he could get to speak with that knight who every day was the first to turn up at the trial of strength. 'That doesn't worry me at all, uncle,' says my lord Gawain. 'Tomorrow I shall be the first to present myself. Then, if he comes as usual, I shall speak with him if he is willing. And, if he's prepared to stop with me, I'll do my best to bring him over.' The maiden pays him great respect and says he will always have her loyal, sincere affection if he can bring him to the king. That was the end of their consultation.

6742   Early next morning my lord Gawain is armed and goes to put
Gringalet* through his paces in the meadows below Jedburgh
and to wait for an opponent to joust with. No one dares come
forward from the ranks to undertake that joust, since they quite
clearly recognise the arms and insignia of the courtly lord
Gawain. One could wait a month before anyone who fought a
personal joust with him would get away with it. There was a very
long wait until hope faded that the man would ever return.
*Then, looking around him, Gawain spied Fergus emerging from
the forest; whereupon he thought and said to himself that he has
no wish at all to joust with him if he can amicably get him to
come – not that he feared him, but he never acted with aggres-
sion unless someone had started it first.

6766   The two noble knights approached each other until they were
able to exchange words. My lord Gawain began by addressing
him, saying: 'My good friend, if I've not challenged you now as
those others did yesterday, don't think me any more cowardly
than they. It's always easy to behave badly. But if for me you
would be kind enough to come and speak with the king, that
would certainly not be to your detriment; for I would be most
grateful to you and would do for you in return anything you
might ask of me.' Fergus replied politely, and said: 'Sir, as God is
my witness, if I were to go with anybody, it would not be for
anyone but you. But now tell me your name as a friend, out of
companionship, and I for my part will go a long way to do as you
advise.' – 'My name was never concealed by me, and I have no
wish to start now. Those who love me and hold me dear call me,
with loyal affection, Gawain, the emperor's nephew. That's my
name, and now you know it. So if you have no strong objection,
tell me yours in return.'

6796   When Fergus hears his very pressing request and knows that
this is lord Gawain, he has no idea what to say, so totally taken
aback is he. All he does is to dismount and run to fling his arms
round his leg, saying: 'Sir, I beg you to forgive me for having
bandied words with you for too long. I am Fergus, who sent the

horn and wimple to King Arthur. If I had recognised you, I'd
have dismounted when I first caught sight of you.' Once my lord
Gawain sees that this is the man he had sought so long and of
whom all the nobles think highly, he dismounts from Gringalet.
Then he unlaces his ventail, and Fergus proceeds to do the same;
and they run forward to kiss each other. You could have walked
slowly for a good four bowshots before they tired of their kiss-
ing: those noble knights made as great a fuss of each other as if
they were full brothers.

6821   The king and all the nobles at court run up at the sight of
such rejoicing. Galiene came too, having witnessed the joyful
scene. The two men take each other by the fingers and, hand in
hand and most joyfully, go to meet the king. Gawain spoke first,
saying to the king: 'My dear good uncle, now you should
rejoice, because, thank God, I've found what you have so longed
for: my dear, beloved companion who has truly won all the
laurels in this tournament; and he certainly should have the
prize, for indeed I never saw a better knight break a lance.
Don't doubt it: this is Fergus; and here and now I ask him for
his love and comradeship.' He embraces Fergus with sincere
affection. The king kisses him on lips and face, with the words:
'Dear good friend, I have yearned for you for a very long time.
I had you sought through many a kingdom, and you may know
that I had this tournament proclaimed in order to find you.
Now I have you, I ask for nothing else; and I've no wish for it to
go on any longer.'*

6851   When the king has made much of Fergus, as had the others,
who were delighted at his arrival, King Arthur with his bare hand
takes Fergus, the amiable Gawain and Galiene alone. Together
with these three he leaves the company and goes to sit under a
juniper tree to discuss and talk of arranging that marriage, and to
find out if he could persuade Fergus willingly to set about taking
that lady as his wife and reigning over Lothian. The king takes
Fergus and embraces him, after which he speaks out, saying:
'Fergus, I have no wish to prevaricate: when I had this tournament

proclaimed, I had it announced through every land that the man who obtained both the victory and the honour in the jousting would have the wife he wished in answer to his best request. You obtained that each day: it's a well-known fact. A lady has come here to me in great need of help. If you wish, I will give her to you; and you shall have the kingdom of Lothian, and I shall increase your domain with the district of Tweeddale,* where there is many a rich residence. You will be powerful and wealthy and will be crowned king at this festival of Saint John, which is to be celebrated tomorrow.'

6887 When Fergus heard the king inviting him to take that lady to wife, he replied: 'Do not ask, but command me as your servant to do what you wish. But I don't know if in any way or manner or circumstance this maiden would wish me to be hers or herself mine. As far as I'm concerned, I wouldn't refuse her if I knew what she wanted.' The king said: 'I know for certain that she will wish it, if you do.' – 'Ask her, then, sire; for otherwise, without knowing her wishes, I wouldn't do it.' Hearing that, the maiden gave a start. And King Arthur appealed to her and said: 'You hear plainly that this man won't refuse anything I choose to order him to do. Are you prepared to agree to do as I wish?' – 'Dear, very good sir, I place at your disposal my mind, my heart, all my sentiments and my entire person.' The king then takes her by the hand and at once bestows her on him who had desired her for so long.*

6917 He has taken possession of his beloved and would not give her up, in brief, for the wealth of Normandy or for the whole empire of Rome. Now he has his beloved; now he is overjoyed. If he loves her, then she loves him three times as much;* if he is handsome, her beauty is as great: no one ever saw the union of two so courtly people. The king raises them by the hands and tells in the hearing of all what he has brought about. Everybody applauds the marriage and, I think, says that with him the lady has made a very good match. With general agreement, the king declares and promises that quite early the next day, before mass is sung, the lady will be crowned. Thus they fixed the time. But, as a result of much pleading, Fergus took with him to Roxburgh the king and all his nobles, his friends and his companions.

6942   It was in fact a Sunday: on that day was celebrated the summer festival dedicated to Saint John. The weather was fine; and that was the day when Fergus wedded his beloved amid much joy and revelry. The town is full of noise and din: drums beat, horns and trumpets resound. Clouds of smoke rise from the kitchens. These were no mock marriage celebrations, for you could hardly move your feet in the town's streets. Fergus sent a messenger straight to the two maidens who were awaiting him in Melrose, for he did not want to leave them out of it. Having heard the news, they come in haste. The town was very full because everybody in the country was there: there were so many people that it was hard to find anywhere in the town to stay. It was a solemn festival, being that of Saint John the Baptist. When the mass had been recited all through and the service was over, then Fergus was crowned, and prudent Galiene as well. Upstairs in the paved hall they hold the great, lavish wedding feast. Never was any seen that was so costly or at which such rich dishes were served: the tables were so laden with them that before two people they placed as much as any six others would eat. Fergus' wedding celebrations lasted for twenty full days, even longer, and were just as excellent on the last as on the first.

6981   Right at the end of the fortnight the king left with his company; and Fergus escorted him as far as the king wished. There was a great commotion when they parted. The courtly lord Gawain embraces and kisses his companion as much as he can, making a fuss of him and urging and begging him not to abandon knightly deeds for his wife, since that is not right. 'For many you'd be a laughing stock!' Fergus swears and gives him his firm assurance that he will never hear of an adventure without heading for it, given good health.* With this they parted. The king leaves, his company with him; and Fergus returned to Roxburgh with his beloved. He is hailed as lord and king, and she as queen. He loves her as his tender sweetheart and she him as her noble lover.

7004   GUILLAUME LE CLERC comes to the end of his subject and his composition. For in no land does he find any man who has lived long enough to be able to tell anything further of the knight with the splendid shield. Here he plants the boundary-stone and post: this is the end of the romance.

7012   May great joy come to those who hear it!

NOTES

The line numbers are those of the Frescoln edition of *Fergus*. For other texts they refer to the editions listed in the Bibliography. The abbreviations *C.I* and *C.II* are used for the First and Second Continuations of the *Perceval*, the section numbers referring to the editorial divisions of those texts.

N.B. The asterisks in the text are placed at the end of the closing line of passages discussed, but at the beginning of sections for which no closing line is given.

1–43 The opening of *Fergus* is a pastiche of that of Chrétien's *Yvain*. There we find King Arthur holding court at Pentecost in Carlisle. After dinner the knights join the ladies to tell anecdotes or talk of love and its blessings and tribulations. A group including Sagremor, Kay, Gawain and Yvain is listening to a companion's account of his adventures when the queen comes upon them unawares. The speaker jumps to his feet with a greeting.

Noticeable in Guillaume's version are the bantering tone and the exclusion of the ladies from the scene, the topic of courtly love being replaced by a show of affection between fellow-knights. As if to advertise his source, he mentions Chrétien's chief heroes, with a special reference to Perceval and his Grail quest.

48–51 In *Erec* King Arthur sets out from his Easter court at Cardigan to renew the custom of hunting the white stag, which he eventually kills himself. Details will suggest, however, that Guillaume owed part of his inspiration for this episode to *C.II* (§§4–5), where it is Perceval who, unusually equipped with a lance, undertakes the hunt and whose hound achieves the capture.

The forest of Gorriende, starting-point of the hunt in *Fergus*, has been tentatively identified by Legge (1950), following Martin, with the district of Geltsdale.

70–75 This is a quirkish modification of the situation in *Erec*, where it is the hero, accompanying the queen to the hunt, whose sumptuous attire includes an ermine mantle.

147 Arthur's enemy, the Chevalier Vermeil, was slain by Perceval when he went to the royal court to seek knighthood.

182–99 The hunt covers much of southern Scotland from the Lammermuirs in the east to the Glasgow district and Galloway in the west, by way of *Aroie*, normally identified as Ayr, though Argyll (to the north and west of Glasgow) has been proposed. *Idegaus* (variants *Indegal, Ingegal*), though probably derived from *Innsi-Gall*, a Celtic name of the Hebrides, evidently means Galloway here. On these names see Frescoln's notes to ll. 188, 194 and 387.

For the bad reputation of the Gallovidians in the Middle Ages, see above, pp xi–xii, and Frescoln's note to ll. 196–99.

236–48 These lines seem to carry ironic echoes of Roland's epic horn-call at Roncevaux (*Chanson de Roland*, ll. 1753–95). In both texts the horn is sounded with great effort and a *longe alaine*; and it is heard from afar by the king, who summons his knights to ride to the caller's assistance. The irony lies in the very different circumstances attending the act and its consequence.

273–80 In *Cligés* Alexander, as his reward for taking the stronghold of the traitor Angrés, receives from Arthur the promised gold cup, which he at once presents to Gawain.

303–13 Pelande seems, for Guillaume, to be an alternative name for Galloway (cf. Frescoln's note to l. 305). The peasant's stronghold has been thought to reflect the poet's familiarity with the primitive Scottish castles of the period, the 'mottes' or earthen mounds topped by wooden buildings within timber palisades.

326 The historical prototype of Soumillet is usually taken to be Somerled, King of Morvern, Lochaber, Argyll and the southern Hebrides and so-called Lord of the Isles. He was distantly related to Fergus of Galloway, being in fact a grandson by marriage (see Legge, 1964).

327–68 In patterning his hero on Perceval, Guillaume nevertheless reverses some elements found in Chrétien's romance. Perceval was the youngest of three brothers: Fergus (as he will later be named) is the eldest of three. Perceval visits his mother's labourers in the fields: Fergus himself ploughs for his father. At the sight of the knights Fergus is terrified, whereas Perceval (despite what the knights thought) was extremely bold.

408 First mentioned by Wace in his *Roman de Brut*, then by Chrétien in *Erec*, the Round Table was destined to become a traditional feature of Arthur's court. Its origins are obscure.

486 Saint Mungo is the popular name of Saint Kentigern. He became Bishop of Glasgow c. 543 and is the city's patron saint.

503 I translate Martin's *ainsnés* ('oldest'; cf. l. 355) rather than the MS reading *puisnés* ('youngest') retained by Frescoln.

537–49 Guillaume is here parodying the situation in *Perceval* where the hero, by appropriating the arms of the Chevalier Vermeil (see the note to l. 147), himself became a 'red knight'.

Brazil wood was a source of red dye, brought from the East.

555–85 The model for the arming of Fergus is *Erec*, ll. 2624–63, where the hero sits on a precious carpet to don armour that includes a magnificent silver hauberk which, Chrétien informs us, was quite rust-proof. Fergus' short, broad sword and sturdy horse have been cited as elements of realism suggesting a knowledge of the Scotland of the day. The *Oxford English Dictionary* defines a galloway as 'one of a small but strong breed of horses peculiar to Galloway'.

588–90 Knights of romance often showed their mettle by leaping into the saddle without the aid of stirrups.

601–4 Perceval left home armed with a javelin; and with it he slew the Chevalier Vermeil.

618–21 Cf. Perceval's mother who, we are told, died of grief at his departure.

644–50 Erec, riding through the countryside with Enide, has two victorious encounters with robber knights on the lookout for booty.

715 Wales was understood as including the British Kingdom of Strathclyde, which originally covered much of north-west England and south-west Scotland.

Perceval, as Fergus here, headed for Carlisle to seek knighthood from Arthur and found him brooding under the challenge of a mortal enemy, in Chrétien's story the Chevalier Vermeil, in Guillaume's the Noir Chevalier. In the following scene Kay's gibes and the jester's prediction are also inspired by *Perceval*.

738–39 Guillaume follows Chrétien's habit of delaying the naming of his chief characters, among them Perceval, whose name is not disclosed until after his climactic adventure at the Grail Castle.

773–93 This adventure is largely developed from elements in *C.II*. There (§5) Perceval fights and defeats a Black Knight in mysterious circumstances. Earlier (§1) he had found a fine horn hanging by a sash from a castle door. On it he gave three great blasts, whereupon he was challenged by a knight, the horn's owner, whose shield was emblazoned with a white lion. Perceval vanquished this Chevalier du Cor and sent him to surrender to Arthur. At his castle he learned of a high mountain, the Mont Dolerous, on whose summit was a marvellous pillar, to which only the finest knight could tether his horse. Perceval set out for the mountain, which he eventually reached (§33), to learn that the pillar had been fashioned long ago by Merlin. The name *la Nouquetran* (variants *Noquetran*, *Noquetrant*) remains unexplained.

825 In *Perceval* (ll. 2796–9) the blond-headed Kay appears with his hair plaited in a tress (*trechiez a une trece*).

864 The Black Mountain is either another name for or, more probably, the site of the Nouquetran, with the latter being the building on its summit. This mountain cannot be positively identified, though several names in the vicinity of Liddel Castle (see the note to ll. 1511–12) contain the element 'black'.

984 The variant in the Paris manuscript is more pungent: *Que ne rengent mauvaise odeur* ('so that they should not give off a foul smell')!

1017 Settled earlier by the Anglo-Saxons, Lothian (eastern Scotland south of the Forth) became the centre of Anglo-Norman influence and culture.

1110–92 The chamberlain plays the role of Gornemant de Gohort in *Perceval* by giving the naïve hero instruction in chivalry. In both cases the young man was under the delusion that, having obtained arms, he was now a knight. Gornemant proceeded to dub Perceval himself; the chamberlain accompanies Fergus to the royal court for the ceremony.

1206–9 Astronomy, one of the Seven Liberal Arts, was portrayed on Erec's coronation robe. The symbolic association here with Fergus' destiny would not be lost on a medieval audience.

1247–9 For physical radiance associated with human beauty cf. *Cligés*, ll. 2749–60, and perhaps *Perceval*, ll. 3224–29, where the brilliance may emanate from the Grail or its bearer.

1338–41 Guillaume makes no attempt to conceal his sources, as this reference to events in *Perceval* shows.

1347–51 In Arthurian romance Gawain is often, as in *Fergus*, an exemplary figure, freely according his companionship to worthy knights, whose standing is thereby enhanced. Perceval was similarly honoured (*Perceval*, ll. 4478 ff.).

1410–14 Symbolically it is Perceval who hands on the sword, the very token of knighthood, to his 'successor'. The donor of the sword to Perceval himself was either Gornemant (although it is not clear that the one with which the knighting was conferred was a gift) or the Fisher King, from whom the hero did receive a precious weapon.

1420 I.e. Yvain.

1463–82 In *Perceval* Kay fells a maiden with a slap then kicks a jester into the fire because of their predictions that the young man would be supreme among knights.

1511–12 The site of Liddel Castle is at Castleton (Borders, formerly Roxburghshire).

The following episode combines features from Perceval's encounters, in Chrétien's romance, with Gornemant de Gohort and Blancheflor who, like the castellan at Liddel and Galiene, are uncle and niece.

1560–61 This conceit and numerous other details are found in Chrétien's descriptions of Enide's beauty in *Erec*, ll. 411–41 and 1484–1516. Guillaume's account could be taken as a humorously exaggerated version of an otherwise conventional description of feminine beauty.

1640 ff. For the account of Love's assault on Galiene, her suffering, self-questioning and sleepless night Guillaume had a model in the first part of *Cligés*. There Soredamors goes through similar agonies and broodings over Alexander (who, unlike Fergus, simultaneously feels love's pangs). But here too Guillaume carries Chrétien's somewhat precious narrative to the point of absurdity, as when he arms Love with a windlass-operated crossbow, or when he later (ll. 1871–77) makes Galiene not merely toss and turn in her bed, but tip it completely over.

1698 I translate Martin's reading *molt tenoit la chiere encline* instead of the variant *bien peüst estre roïne* adopted by Frescoln. Galiene, like Soredamors, is trying to hide her feelings.

1890 ff. Galiene's action is inspired by Blancheflor's nocturnal visit to Perceval's bed in Chrétien's work. There are, however, significant differences between the two scenes. It is ironic that, whereas Galiene wishes Fergus to abandon his perilous adventure, Blancheflor's secret desire is to inspire Perceval to fight against her besiegers. Moreover, unlike Galiene, she achieves her end; for Perceval draws her into his bed with reassuring words and next day insists on taking up her cause.

1987–8 Frescoln unnecessarily inverts these two lines. I take *se blasmer de* as the antonym of *se löer de* ('express satisfaction with').

2000–16 When Galiene abruptly abandons her stance as a typical despairing courtly lover and decides out of family pride to accept her father's marriage plans for her and have done with love, Guillaume again seems to be mocking courtly love conventions.

2087 The olive tree, with its symbolic connotations, frequently appears in the romances as it does, often more realistically, in the epics. In *Fergus* other examples are found at Roxburgh (l. 5190) and Carlisle (l. 6191). In *C.II* Perceval fights the Chevalier du Cor (see note to ll. 773–93 above) beside an olive tree (variant: almond tree).

2119–21 From the heights in the area of Liddel Castle there are extensive views embracing parts of northern England and the Irish Sea (the Solway Firth), but the mention of Cornwall is poetic licence, giving a convenient rhyme.

2129 ff. In *C.II* (§5) Perceval has to summon the Black Knight by going to an arched, hermitage-like 'tomb' (by a marble cross in one version) and addressing the painted figure of a knight. This seems to have been Guillaume's inspiration for his chapel with its inanimate guardian. From the episode of the Chevalier du Cor (see note to ll. 773–93) he appears to have taken the further details of the white lion (painted in *C.II*, sculptured in *Fergus*), horn and wimple (sash in *C.II*). If this is the case, we have here a good example of Guillaume's technique of selecting elements from different places and blending them, with a touch of wry humour, into a lively new scene.

2235–38 In *C.II* (§1) Perceval similarly alerted the Chevalier du Cor with three mighty blasts on the horn.

2589 *Eschoce* (*Escoche*) meant at this time the part of modern Scotland north of the Forth.

2634 ff. Like Galiene earlier, Fergus now suffers the torments of the courtly lover before standing back and considering his situation rationally. Then, however, he consciously opts for the conventional role, despite his host's disapproval. The scene thus has the ingredients of a debate on the place of courtly love and even of love itself in the knight's life. We are left to decide, here as elsewhere, whether Guillaume's gentle mockery veils a serious commentary on the courtly manners and attitudes of his day.

2806 ff. The next section of the romance sees Guillaume turning from *Perceval* to *Yvain* as his chief source of inspiration. Yvain, on being rejected by Laudine, took to the forests and there spent a long period of physical and mental destitution. The love-lorn wanderings of Fergus are, however, punctuated by bouts of chivalric activity, of which the first, his encounter with the knight in the tent, is based on an episode in *C.II* (§9). There Perceval finds a lion guarding a tent in which are a knight and his mistress. Perceval kills the lion and wakes the maiden, whose cries alert the knight. He complains of the attack on his guard, has the maiden call for his arms, then fights a losing combat with the hero, who despatches him and his *amie* to Arthur's court.

In substituting a dwarf for the lion, Guillaume may have remembered a similar episode in *C.I* (§§VI.3–4), where the tent is defended by a remarkably handsome dwarf knight. The hide-ousness of his own dwarf (ll. 2828–37) could be an instance of his characteristic reversal technique, but is also evidently patterned on the appearance of Chrétien's giant herdsman (another reversal) in *Yvain*, ll. 288–313.

2874 Friesland has long been noted for its manufacture of fine cloth.

2900–18 The legal terminology used here and elsewhere in the romance might suggest that Guillaume had special interests in this field.

3041–44 Fortune is commonly represented in medieval school tradition as having hair in front but none at the back of her head.

3172 This is the only place where Fergus' first horse is named.

3243 ff. The courtly ideal is again undermined when Fergus' hunger overcomes his love-sickness. In *C.II* (§20) Perceval was plagued by hunger, having, like Fergus, had no food for two days.

The ensuing events in Guillaume's work seem, however, to travesty an episode in *C.I* (§IV.3). There Arthur and fifteen of his company are suffering from hunger, when Kay comes across a dwarf roasting a peacock on a spit. When the bird is denied him, Kay sends the dwarf flying with a kick. Thereupon a knight appears, complains of Kay's behaviour, and deals him a great blow with the charged spit. Later, however, the knight entertains Arthur and his companions handsomely. With typical irony, Guillaume has turned the king's fifteen famished knights into fifteen feasting rogues, of whom the eventual survivors are sent as captives to the royal court.

3426 *Se Dius le noviel chevalier*: I take this to be a scribal error for *Seviaus* ('at least') *le n. ch.* Martin prints *Que vostre n. ch.*

3550 *Les mors as mors, les vis as vis*: in Chrétien's romance (l. 3630) Perceval spoke the same words shortly after learning of his mother's death.

3655 ff. Fergus' means of survival and pitiful state are modelled on those of the deranged Yvain. But whereas the latter was cured through human agency, Fergus owed his rehabilitation to the rejuvenating properties of a marvellous spring. Guillaume doubtless had in mind the magic, storm-producing spring of Brocéliande in *Yvain* (both have a chapel close by), though its attributes are those of the traditional Fountain of Youth.

3753 ff. The Dunnottar adventure will be Fergus' supreme test, the equivalent of Perceval's Grail quest, which was only begun in Chrétian's romance and not fully achieved in the Continuations. The shining shield is, then, Guillaume's substitute for the Grail. He appears to have found its prototype in *C.II* (§29), where Gawain discovers a silver shield hanging on a tree near which a beautiful maiden sits combing her hair beside a spring. Its guardian, a dwarf knight, tells Gawain that it can only be carried by a knight of outstanding merit who has a faithful, loving mistress. Any other will be promptly unhorsed; but its worthy bearer will have his strength and virtues doubled. We recognise the bright, protective, talismanic shield and its

association with the hero's beloved, as explained by a prescient
dwarf; and we suspect another of Guillaume's reversal tricks in
the transmogrification of the lovely, golden-haired maiden plying
her comb into the shaggy, scythe-wielding hag at Dunnottar. The
equation of the shield with the Grail also brings to mind that
other radiant maiden, its customary bearer.

The reasons for Guillaume's choice of Dunnottar (Grampian
region) for Fergus' goal are obscure; but it is an appropriately
dramatic site, accurately described in ll. 3848–59. The present
castle ruins date from the late 14th century, though the rock
carried more primitive fortifications from prehistoric times as
well as a succession of chapels from the 5th century onwards.

3782–92 Fergus' irreverent declaration, showing courtly love
at its most extreme and amoral, may well have inspired the more
familiar words of Aucassin in the *chantefable* (*Aucassin et
Nicolette*, VI.24–39).

3898–903 Fergus has now achieved that balance between love
and chivalry which is the ideal finally attained by Chrétien's Erec
and Yvain.

3929 A common medieval name for Edinburgh.

3934 ff. Queen Margaret of Scotland gave her name to
Queensferry, a favourite crossing-point on the Firth of Forth,
where a ferry plied for over eight hundred years until the building
of the [first] road bridge. For Lothian and Scotland see the notes
to ll. 1017 and 2589.

Fergus' affray with the boatmen may have been suggested by
an incident in *C.II* (§3), when a maiden offers to ferry Perceval
over a river, but with the intention of drowning him. A friendly
boatman warns him, then performs the service himself.

4051–52 This is probably the stronghold occupied in the 11th
century by Malcolm III (Canmore), whose queen, the Saxon
Margaret (see the previous note) founded Scotland's first
Benedictine abbey. The epithet *sarrasin*, which I have translated
as 'outlandish', has been taken to refer to the primitive motte-
and-bailey structures of the period (see note to ll. 303–13),

though it may simply be a convenient rhyme for *Dunfremelin*. Dunfermline lies about three miles north of the Forth.

4058–95 In *C.I* (§V.3) Gawain rides along a causeway stretching into the sea as he makes for a mysterious, fiery brilliance. It comes, in fact, from the Grail Castle, which he enters. This strengthens our impression that Dunnottar was Guillaume's 'alternative' Grail Castle.

4210–317 Some of the details of this scene are unclear. With the lurking dragon roused by Fergus we may compare the serpent in *C.I* (§III.11) which attacks a knight who opens a cupboard in which it is concealed. The dragon mentioned as having been slain by Tristan (ll. 4215–16) had ravaged the lands of the Irish king, Yseult's father.

4412–54 The siege of Roxburgh, Galiene's castle, is inspired by that of Blancheflor's stronghold, Belrepeire, in Chrétien's *Perceval*. Belrepeire had suffered a long siege by the seneschal Engygeron and his master Clamadeu des Illes, who coveted the castle and Blancheflor herself, when Perceval came to her rescue. Galiene is in a similar situation, her father having died a year previously (see ll. 6658–59). It is not clear whether the king now besieging her is the one to whom her father had wished to marry her (ll. 1842–43), an arrangement to which she had seemed resigned (ll. 2012–13).

The ruins of Roxburgh Castle lie between the Tweed and the Teviot, three miles from the present village of that name (Borders region).

4460 ff. *Mont Dolerous*, which also appears in *C.II* (see note to ll. 773–93 above), is here associated with Melrose and is probably to be identified with the nearby Eildon Hills, the site of the Roman fort of Trimontium. The giant's castle is later referred to (l. 4753) as *Li Chastiaus de la Roce Bise*.

The source of this episode is in *C.II* (§12), where Perceval seeks lodging in the riverside fortress of a giant, who holds a maiden in a pitiful condition because she will not surrender to him. Perceval slays the giant after the latter has killed his horse with a club; but he replaces the animal with a splendid steed he finds in a cellar, where it has been kept in prime condition. He leaves the rescued maiden, who attends him well, in charge of the castle on his departure.

4523–641 The combat itself contains some reminiscences of Yvain's fight with the giant Harpin de la Montagne, for instance the severing of the shoulders from the trunk and the crash of the giant's fall being compared with that of a toppling oak (*Fergus*, ll. 4616–19, 4640–41; *Yvain*, ll. 4238–47). Guillaume also seems to have had in mind Roland's slaying of the giant Ferracutus (Ferracut, Fernagut) as related in the very popular *Pseudo-Turpin Chronicle*. That giant, having picked up other knights and carried them off bodily, was engaged by Roland, whose horse he killed at a blow. As they grappled on foot, Roland managed to take Ferracutus' sword and pierce him through the navel, his only vulnerable spot. (See the Old French version edited by Ronald N. Walpole, §XVII).

4790 Roxburgh Castle is some ten miles from Melrose as the crow flies.

5218–19 The reference to Wasselin and his messengers is obscure.

5258–66 In *Yvain* Lunete, charged with treason by having engineered her mistress' marriage to the hero, rashly offered to find a champion to fight in her defence against her three accusers.

5324 *Sens vaut molt mius que estoutie*. Compare Oliver's reproof of Roland: '*Mielz valt mesure que ne fait estultie*' (*Chanson de Roland*, l. 1725). Guillaume's knowledge of the council and embassy scenes in the *Roland* may have coloured this section of the romance.

5339 ff. Arondele's mission on behalf of her mistress has much in common with that of the disinherited sister and her messenger in *Yvain*, the object being in both cases to find a knight to champion the lady in a judicial combat.

5384–411 In *C.II* (§28) many of Arthur's knights, including Gawain, Kay, Sagremor, Erec and Lancelot, leave court to search for the missing Perceval. For the identification of the place names in this section, see Frescoln's note to l. 5397.

5433 *Galvoie* could be Galway in Ireland, or Galloway. Frescoln justifies the translation 'Galway' in his note to this line.

5662–63 In *Perceval* Blancheflor, when she comes to Perceval's bed, expresses the same intention.

5768–80 In *Erec* Enide, thinking her husband dead, was about to take her own life, when God in His mercy sent a party of people to prevent the act. Galiene is also deterred by a seemingly supernatural agency. For other examples of heroines contemplating suicide, see Frescoln, p. 26.

In *C.II* (§22) Perceval sees a light so brilliant that the forest, as in *Fergus*, appears on fire: it in fact comes from the Grail. Here again we find an equation of shining shield and Grail.

5788–801 Even this unusual detail seems inspired by *C.II*. There (§29), less than thirty lines before Gawain discovers the silver shield (see note to ll. 3753 ff. above), we learn how he was wet through by the unusually heavy morning dew.

5842–45 I have found no reference elsewhere to such a custom, which is probably fictitious.

6029–49 In *Perceval* the vanquished Clamadeu had refused to give himself up to Blancheflor, but proceeded instead to Arthur's court. Here the defeated king does take Fergus' message to Galiene, now queen (see ll. 6658–59), on his way to the same destination.

6149 ff. The account of the king's arrival is modelled on that of Clamadeu's surrender at the royal court in *Perceval*. Arthur's company has now returned to court as anticipated in ll. 5405–11.

Arthur's curious occupation of whittling a stick (ll. 6176–77), earlier indulged in by Gawain (ll. 1325–27), was in Chrétien's *Perceval* ascribed to a mysterious figure with an artificial leg seated on a bundle of rushes (ll. 7656–59).

6296 ff. The tournament at Jedburgh has its chief model in *C.II* (§24), where Perceval, incognito like Fergus, jousts successfully with some of Arthur's leading knights (including Lancelot), toppling Kay, who had requested the initial encounter, and withdrawing to the forest at the end of the first day but returning on the morrow. Gawain tries to discover the identity of both heroes, but succeeds only in the case of Fergus. For other parallels in Chrétien's *Cligés* and *Lancelot* see Frescoln, p. 27.

6344–79 Galiene follows Laudine's example in *Yvain* (ll. 2038 ff.) by manipulating her lords in council to advise a course of action, namely to take a husband, which she would in any case have adopted.

6416–17 In *Yvain* we learn that Kay would be granted any joust he requested, unless Gawain asked first (ll. 683–88); and in fact he later obtains this privilege.

6450 These are common names of horses, usually black (Morel, Morial) or white (Flori). See Frescoln's note to this line.

6592–95 Guillaume had earlier assured us (ll. 1427–29) that Fergus would prove second in valour to Gawain alone. The common opinion here that this honour belongs to Perceval reinforces the point that Fergus is about to supersede him.

6664–65 *Bien a un mois, que le savés. / Bataille en prist anvers le roi.* In place of these lines, I translate the variant reading:

> Si que vous molt bien le savés.
> Passé a plus de quarante dis
> Que ma pucele vous tramis
> Pour querre secours et aïe.
> Mais a la court ne trouva mie
> Nus de chiaus que ele queroit.

6745 Gringalet (usually, as here, *le Gringalet*) was well known as Gawain's horse. The name may derive from Welsh *ceincaled* ('handsome-hardy') or possibly *guin-calet* ('white-hardy').

6758 ff. Gawain was celebrated for his civility and powers of persuasion. Chrétien shows him exercising these on the hero in *Erec* (ll. 4076 ff.), and in *Perceval* (ll. 4349 ff.), where he also shows his traditional readiness to disclose his name.

6815–50 The extravagant display of affection by both Gawain and Arthur deflects our attention from the reunion of the lovers, which would be the conventional climax of the romance. Whether this betrays a misogynous streak in Guillaume's character or simply continues his playful mockery of the courtly love conventions is a matter for debate.

6881 Tweeddale was the popular name for Peeblesshire, now in the Borders region. Roxburgh Castle stood at the confluence of the Tweed and the Teviot.

6887–916 In *Cligés* (ll. 2269–349) Queen Guenevere plays the role of match-maker here assumed by Arthur when she brings together Alexander and Soredamors. It is noticeable that Fergus does not, like Alexander, profess undying love regardless of the lady's attitude. Galiene and Soredamors both place themselves entirely at the disposal of the king and queen respectively.

6922 This statement of the degree of their mutual love is ironically the reverse of that between Lancelot and Guenevere (*Lancelot*, ll. 4680–81), for Chrétien tells us that if he was dear to the queen, his love for her was a hundred thousand times as great!

6986–95 Similar advice is given by Gawain in his persuasion of Yvain to leave his new wife for a while to go tourneying (*Yvain*, ll. 2484–538). As well as warning against the danger of degenerating in marriage, he argues that absence makes the heart grow fonder, a positive point not found in *Fergus*. Guillaume's public would be well aware that in Yvain's case this advice led to the almost fatal breakdown of his marriage–a worrying thought to prompt at the conclusion of his romance, and no doubt a parting thrust at the courtly love ideal.

APPENDIX A

Fergus and the Continuations

This appendix contains, in translation, the principal episodes from the *Perceval* Continuations used by Guillaume le Clerc for his pastiche (see my article 'The Craft of *Fergus*: Supplementary Notes'). Most are taken from the second of these, in which Perceval plays the leading role; but some figure among Gawain's adventures in the Second Continuation. The material is presented in the order in which Guillaume made use of it. The headings refer to events in his romance and the line numbers to the points at which they are discussed in the Notes.

The hunting of the white stag (48–51)

Perceval makes advances to a maiden, who initially rejects them.

'But if you wish to enjoy my love, it will be necessary for you to go into a park near here and hunt the white stag with might and main so you manage to catch it: you'll not have to be half-hearted in the hunt. If you bring me its head, I'll then do as you wish, without any objections. And you shall take my little hunting dog with you: he's so good that once he's caught sight of the quarry, there's no chance of his ever losing it. Take very good care of this hound for me, because I wouldn't have him lost on any account. Lose him, and you'd certainly never have my love. And you'll go fully armed, so as not to get into trouble.' – 'As you say, my fair one,' says he. 'Let's have the hound! Hand him over to me, and I'll waste no time before doing just as you've told me.'

The damsel at once rose to her feet and went into her room, but without staying there long. She came back with her hound, not looking in the least disconsolate. The dog, which was on a long leash embroidered with gold, was as white as snow. The damsel offered it to Perceval, who took it most willingly and gladly and went off with it down the stairs; but whether he returns is in God's hands. He came to the foot of a tower, where his horse was ready for him. At once he mounted, his shield at his neck and a lance in his grasp; and without more ado he left, taking with him neither bow nor arrows.

He went on until he came to the park and started searching for his stag. In half a league of open ground he found it completely on its own. With a halloo he immediately released his hound; and I tell you truly that the dog brought it down on a rock by sheer strength and force. Seeing the stag caught, Perceval wasted no time in getting there; and, quite overjoyed, he dismounted and promptly took off its head. (*C. II*, §§ 4–5, Mss *ET*, ll. 20263–316)

The Black Knight adventure (773–93, 2129 ff)

(a) *Perceval has ridden for two days without food or drink.*

He saw in the middle of the heath ahead a fine, strong castle. There were no cottages or houses visible, but just the outer enclosure with white walls, new and lofty, quite safe from the danger of assault. Round them was no moat, only good land and attractive meadows. Above the gateway stood a magnificent tower, but there were no other towers or turrets. In it was set a gate of ebony. As soon as Perceval saw it, he thought and said to himself that the castle seemed to be situated in a very desolate spot. He continued on until he arrived in front of it, but without finding there any living creature. He at once rode all round it until he was back at the entrance, where he saw the gate tightly shut. For a long while he gazed at it, because never before in all his days had he set eyes on one so beautiful or showing such rich workmanship; for the lock and all of its bars and fastenings were of pure, red Spanish gold. At its centre was set a massive ring of chased gold.

From this ring, my lords, there hung by a sash of precious gilt brocade an ivory horn that was whiter than snow or any lily. It was banded with fine red gold and most richly decorated. On seeing it, Perceval says may God never help him if he should leave that place before he has blown the horn. He immediately takes off his helmet and, with his face freed of its armour, fixes his eyes on that horn. Waiting no longer, he forthwith takes it and on it gives such a powerful, loud, clear blast that the countryside around reverberates to the horn's sound.

Once he had sounded it, he did not have long to wait before he heard, it seemed to him, people moving about in the castle and talking, and one man saying: 'Did you hear that? The horn here never sounded like that before. Whoever blew it with such vigour is a person to be reckoned with!' Then he said: 'Quick! Have my armour brought, so I can put it on.' Hearing that, Perceval was quite amazed by the words that were spoken, since he could see nothing of the speaker. Then he looked through an opening beside one of the gate hinges and saw a young man pass by carrying a shield, its blazon resplendent with gules and a huge ermine lion, its neck-strap entirely of gold brocade and those for the arms of costly Grecian silk: its fittings were the height of elegance. The youth bearing the shield went into a hall. Perceval, I can assure you, would have liked to hold that shield outside the gate, having seen its great beauty.

He stayed a long while by the gate completely on his own. After some time he took the horn and sounded it again, louder and more clearly than before. Then immediately he heard a man say: 'I have indeed heard a wonderful thing, thanks be to God! The best knight in the world, endowed with the highest prowess, has blown the horn: I'm sure of it. And I'll put him to the test this very day.' After that, he said no more. But Perceval put all his strength into a third mighty blast.

Thereupon he saw a knight emerge from the hall, armed and astride a swift charger which was entirely covered with a cloth of bright red samite: never did any man see a better. He was followed by many knights, youths, men-at-arms and squires. Then, whether for good or ill, the gate was quickly opened. When Perceval spied them, he retreated back into the meadow and took his stand under an olive tree, there to await the knight. The latter rushed out through the gate in his extremely handsome armour. A crown he wore firmly attached to his helmet suited him wonderfully: it was covered with gems of many kinds, and much care must have been devoted to its creation. It signified that he was a king, the lord of Ireland and Norway.

Once he was outside, the shield carried by Perceval and the steed he rode were recognised in many quarters. The king was grief-stricken and said with great affection: 'Dear Lord God, what has become of my friend? What country is he in? Since I sent him to Britain, I've had no sure news of him. Those are his arms I can see there, but I don't know who that man is with them. Now I'm convinced he's either a captive or dead; and I can't be blamed if I grieve for him.' So saying, he entered the meadow with a challenge for Perceval; and he returned it, recognising him now as an enemy.

After a savage combat the Knight of the Horn is forced to submit to Perceval, who spares him on condition that, once his wounds are healed, he go to constitute himself King Arthur's prisoner. Both men are then taken into the castle, where they remain until fully recovered.

When that day came, news reached them that on the lofty summit of the Dolorous Mount was a marvellous pillar studded all about with pure gold nails. But there was no man born of woman who could on any account tether his steed to it unless, at the time he made the attempt, he were peerless in arms above all others in the world. Immediately Perceval heard that, he said without hesitation: 'True God, what am I doing here? I shall indeed never rest until I know for sure whether I am a worthy or a base man. Day and night I shall continue on until I'm able to reach that pillar: then I shall learn for certain whether I shall be a good knight.' (C.II, § 1, Mss *AKLMQSU*, ll. 9531–664, 9818–39)

(b) *On his way to the Dolorous Mount Perceval has many adventures. After he has cut off the head of the white stag (see above), a damsel appears, claims that the beast was hers, and seizes the hound, which she at first refuses to return.*

'But go to that archway over there, and you will find a tomb on which there is a painting of a knight. Just ask him straight away: "Vassal, what are you doing here?" Then, I promise you, you'll have the hound.' Perceval was quick to reply: 'I'll not be the loser for such a trifle.' Then he took the head and set off for the arch without wasting time, since he was quite sure of the way. He saw there a cross and the tomb in which were four openings, as in a kind of cell. Then Perceval called aloud: 'Sir knight, so help me God, whoever put you in this tomb was wasting his time. Get up: you've lain there too long!'

Looking round, he saw behind him a fully armed knight on his charger; and his armour was blacker by far than a ripe blackberry. And what could I tell you? This knight at once asked him: 'What do you want, sir vassal? That was very wicked and rash of you. It was exceedingly arrogant of you to call me, but unlucky for you to have thought of doing so.' With that he drew back in order to launch an assault on him. (C. II, § 5, Mss *AKLMPQSU*, ll. 10217–247)

After a bitter combat, during which an interloper makes off with the hound and the head, the Black Knight is defeated and retreats into his tomb, whence Perceval fails to summon him again. He concludes that he has been bewitched.

(c) Perceval eventually arrives at the foot of the Dolorous Mount. There a maiden warns him of its perils, but fails to break his resolve.

Perceval bridled his horse, mounted, and rode alone up to the summit of the Dolorous Mount. He examined the pillar and its admirable workmanship: it was, I think, entirely fashioned of copper and gilded over so that it shone from top to bottom, being a bowshot high. Around it stood fifteen crosses, not one of which was less than a hundred and twenty feet tall. I do not believe that human eyes ever beheld any work as beautiful, as we are told by the full written account at Fécamp. Perceval was quite astounded by the sight of these great marvels. Of the fifteen crosses five were scarlet, five whiter than snow fallen on branches, and the others in fact of a lovely shade of blue, all of them in natural hues. They were made of hard stone that would last for ever. Perceval passed by these superb crosses and let his eyes wander on the splendid tall pillar with its gilding. He noticed a ring attached to it, I am not sure whether of silver or gold, but worth all the treasure that a tower could hold. Around it, on a fine silver band, was an inscription entirely in Latin, saying that no knight should presume to tether his steed to the pillar unless he could measure up to the best knight of all those at present in the world. Though Perceval could not read it, he had heard all about it from that knight he had met who had pushed him into the tomb and had told him all the particulars. Dismounting, he took his reins and tied them to the ring and, that done, left his steed standing there quietly. Against this same pillar he leant his shield and with it his sharp, steel-tipped lance. There he stood quite still and took off his helmet to listen for any sound and watch for anything that might happen. Then suddenly there appeared a maiden riding a white mule.

This maiden greeted him as the greatest of knights. She named herself as the Damsel of the High Peak of the Dolorous Mount. Although she spoke of her magnificent castle not far away, she entertained him in a nearby tent, where she told him the history of this place. Long ago, Merlin had promised King Utherpendragon to disclose a test whereby he might identify the finest knight in his land.

'At that, Merlin immediately left the court and rode off through great woods, over mountains, across heaths and plains, travelling this way and that, high and low, until he came across this lofty peak. He then began to apply his cunning and magic arts until he created the crosses and the pillar. My mother was then still youthful, no more than twenty. She turned up here and acted foolishly, being unable to leave him when she intended to go away: instead she did as he wished and became his mistress. For her he built the beautiful residence I've just told you about. When the time came for him to return to Utherpendragon, he found him at Caerleon, which is in Wales. There in his halls he told his story in the presence of a hundred or more knights, kings, counts and dukes among them: how he had found a pillar to which none could tether his horse, other than the best man in his whole domain. On hearing that, the king was delighted. He took there numerous excellent knights of high reputation, but they came to grief. Merlin left the court and came to live with my mother, upon whom he fathered me. You should not doubt my word for this, because the story I've told you is as true as the Paternoster.' (*C. II*, § 33, Mss *EKLMPQSTUV*, ll. 31580–641, 31872–909)

The knight in the tent (2806 ff.)

From the window of a deserted castle Perceval sees a beautiful enclosed meadow where, beside a fountain, is the most splendid tent he has ever seen.

Before the tent stood a tree, a cypress as we read, which at all seasons had a sweet fragrance. Right at its foot there lay a great strong, bold lion, stretched out beneath it. Perceval took a good look at it, then resolved to go to the tent to see if he would find anyone there. [*He cannot find his horse where he had left it, but takes up his shield, finds his way into the meadow and, with drawn sword, makes for the tent.*]

The lion heard him, jumped to its feet and, rearing forward with great ferocity, came running at Perceval. With its claws it struck at his scarlet shield. Perceval's alarm is no surprise to me, for it dragged the shield down from his neck, tearing apart its strap of silk decorated with gold leaf. But Perceval was undismayed: he aimed a great sword-blow at its head, sparing no effort, and splitting it apart with his steel blade. Thus he dealt with the lion.

He hurried on to the tent and entered at once. On his way in he encountered a lovely, fair-complexioned maiden. She saw him grasping his naked sword and cried in terror: 'Help, Holy Mary, help!' As the maiden was calling out, Perceval looked across and saw a knight lying in a bed on a precious silk coverlet. He had been wakened by the din; and you may be sure he was very worried by the cries of his beloved and the sight of this armed man right in the middle of his tent, holding in his hand his naked, bloody sword.

'Vassal,' he said, 'your coming in here is the height of insolence! That was certainly great folly on your part, which you'll repent too late.' Then he leapt furiously to his feet. And Perceval said to him: 'You might have been much more polite, good sir. If I arrived here with drawn sword, it was no insult to you: I came in because I needed a lodging, nothing more: that's why I entered this tent. But in the meadow I saw a huge, ugly lion that attacked me; and I defended myself against it. So I killed it, to my great delight. That's the reason my sword was drawn.'

– 'Indeed!' exclaimed the knight, who was extremely proud and arrogant, bad-tempered and irate. 'Who ordered you to kill my lion, of which I was so fond? If God grant me health and happiness, I'll take good vengeance on you for that. Here! My arms for me to put on! Don't waste time, damsel! Quick, call two lads!' – 'Certainly,' she replies, and then calls two squires, who lose no time in coming before their lord. He bids them saddle his horse and have his hauberk, shield and lance fetched. 'And one of them is to hurry at once to bring this vassal his horse immediately.'

His orders were carried out: they brought Perceval his horse, and he mounted immediately. Then the knight, determined to avenge his shameful killing of his lion, declared and swore that Perceval was now in dire straits. With that he armed himself and mounted the charger that was led out for him. It was almost sunset when they were both on their horses; and you should know that Perceval had taken up a stout lance with a sharp steel tip, which he had found by the entrance to the tent. They had no mind to swap more words or ask for anything further, but gave their steeds their head on a free rein, spurring them as hard as they could. (*C. II*, § 9, Mss *EKLMPQSTU*, ll. 21125–33, 21163–252)

There ensues a vicious fight, at first with lances and then with swords, which ends with the tent-knight's defeat and his pledging to go to submit to King Arthur.

The disputed meal (3243 ff.)

With fifteen of his knights King Arthur sets out for a distant castle to rescue another member of his company.

With those fifteen the king journeyed on and, I believe, passed through the land of Brittany, riding hard. One day the king, without having eaten, emerged from a great forest onto a broom-covered heath. The hot sun blazed down on this vast, barren heath. What with the heat and his lack of food, the king was so exhausted that he needed to rest, if a pleasant spot could be found. By chance they found a tall tree, beneath which was a spring; and there they halted. Because of the heat and their fatigue, they removed the armour from their hands and heads and washed their faces and their mouths. I am sure they were all in sore need of food, but, as I say, they had none; and they were distressed for the sake of the king, who was suffering badly from his fast.

In the middle of the heath, far down below the forest, my lord Gawain spotted and pointed out to the seneschal a well-thatched dwelling. 'Kay,' he said, 'it seems to me there are folk in that cottage.' – 'That's true,' said Kay. 'I'll go there to see if I can find provisions: just wait here for me.'

In the house Kay found an old woman, who directed him to a richly endowed but apparently deserted castle, which he entered.

He went into a very long, wide, high hall; and on a broad hearth he saw a splendid fire blazing. However, he found nobody there other than a single dwarf, who was roasting a very plump peacock. Never was a finer one seen: it was excellently larded and on a great apple-wood spit, which the dwarf was expert at turning.

Kay hurried forward and met a surly reception. 'Dwarf,' said the seneschal, 'tell me if there's anyone but you in here.' The fellow refused to utter a word. Kay would have killed him without more ado, had he not feared it would have brought shame on him; but he knew that would certainly have been extremely base of him. 'You wicked, hunchbacked dwarf,' he said, 'I can't see anyone in this house except you and this peacock that I'll have now for my dinner. And those I want to share it with will definitely get some too.' – 'So help me that King who doesn't lie,' said the dwarf, 'you'll never eat any of it and won't share it around either. I advise you to quit this place, or else you can rest assured that you'll soon be kicked out.'

Kay was really annoyed at that and stepped forward to strike him; and with a kick he promptly sent him sprawling against the pillar of the fireplace so that the hearth was covered in blood. Because of the heat of the fire the dwarf crossed himself and screamed out, for he was terrified he was going to die. Then the seneschal heard to his left a door flung open with a loud bang, and through it came a knight who was very tall, strong and fierce as well as exceedingly handsome and good-looking; and he was no more than thirty years old. He wore a tunic of new silk lined with ermine for warmth, not long, but wide and ample: he was most tastefully dressed. His breeches were very elegant; and I tell you truly that he had a beautiful belt with gold rings more costly than would be found in any treasury. He entered hatless and seemed quite perturbed. He was followed by a greyhound which he held by a fine silken collar.

On seeing the dwarf bleeding, he did not hesitate, but said at once: 'You, who've come up here fully armed into this hall, why have you knocked my servant down?' Kay's reply was prompt: 'A curse on this servant now, for in the world there's none so villainous or tiny or deformed!' – 'By all the saints,' retorted the knight, 'that's slander I hear!' – 'You're one to complain, my good sir,' the seneschal replied: 'I've seen many smart vassals quite as noble as you: you're just a disagreeable churl. What's this fine talk of yours if I did strike that fellow who was roasting the peacock?' His rejoinder was civil: 'You're not very polite, sir. But, in God's name, I've a small favour to ask: that you consent to tell me your name.' Kay replied furiously: 'I'll be very glad to tell you: I've told it to five hundred better knights than you, so help me God. You shall know the truth: my name's Kay.' – 'Indeed, sir, I should well believe that this is the pure truth, for you're recognisable at once, merely from your speech. So the lad refused you the peacock. In my house it's not the custom to refuse food to anyone who has asked for it. You shall have your share of the peacock very soon. God save me!'

With that he took it along with the spit, then heaved it up, striking Kay a mighty, violent blow with it, almost killing him. And do you know where he caught him? On the neck, so that he toppled him over without a sound leg to hold him up. As the turkey burst apart, the fat from it ran through the mesh of his hauberk; and afterwards, for every day of his life, my lord Kay bore a very ugly mark from the incident up his neck as far as his ear. Then the knight tossed the peacock to his two greyhounds, saying: 'Get up, Sir Kay: that was your share, and you'll get no more. For God's sake get out of my sight! It makes me very angry to see you.' Then there arrived two well armed servants, who led him away. (C. I, § IV. 3, Mss *TVD*, ll. 9198–231, 9268–386)

Kay returns crestfallen and tells his tale to the king, who there-upon sends his nephew to the castle. Gawain is received with the utmost courtesy; and Arthur and his company are welcomed by its lord to a lavish feast.

The shining shield (3753 ff.)

Gawain has left Arthur's court in search of Perceval and with the intention of learning, if possible, the secrets of the Grail. Early one day he is riding through a great forest.

It was a very dull morning; and there was so much dew that it dripped like heavy rain from the tall trees on every side. Gawain was quite drenched. But the sun broke through to disperse the mist, and it grew warm and so bright that there had not been so fine a day during the whole of that month. On rode Gawain with-out a break, his spirits raised by such beautiful weather and by the sound of the small birds, who were singing so loud and clear that they seemed to him to be talking as they sang, and reciting in their own tongue the tale of their love. At that Sir Gawain began to reflect deeply that no one, hearing those birds, could refrain or keep his heart from loving, so very sweetly did they sing.

As he was immersed in these thoughts as his only preoccupation, he looked ahead and saw a great tall, leafy tree; and hanging from one of its branches there was a shield. I have no doubt at all that the shield was of silver; and it bore a handsome young lion rampant, completely black. Beneath the tree, to tell the truth, was a beautiful clear, limpid spring, with a stream running down from it.

Sir Gawain rode his horse straight to this little spring; and seated there he saw a maiden, wearing an ermine mantle. In her bare white hand she held an ivory comb, with which she was combing her hair quite alone, attended by no servant or maid. Yet so fair and attractive was she that no one more beautiful has been born. Her complexion was so very delicate with a flush of crimson on the white that my lord Gawain had the impression that this was actually a statue; and he would certainly have firmly believed that, had she remained sitting quietly without moving. But he saw her combing and smoothing down her hair, which had the appearance of gold; and from this he knew for certain that she was a damsel or lady. He swore to himself that this side of Rome there was no woman or girl or damsel more beautiful.

Gawain and the maiden quickly feel a mutual attraction. There then appears a handsome but diminutive knight. He is the girl's brother and offers Gawain hospitality. They prepare to leave for the dwarf knight's castle.

Then Gawain asked him if the shield hanging there was to be left on that branch. The Little Knight replied: 'By all the saints in the world, my lord, no knight should take it to bear or hang at his neck without having a great deal of intelligence, strength and vigour, generosity, nobility and honour. He should, moreover, have a beautiful mistress, who has nothing base about her but is loyal, loving him as her own heart, who would on no account wish ill to befall him any more than to herself, and would take no joy in any other lover, however great his renown. The man to

whom God granted such a destiny could well bear this shield and
bestow it wherever he wished; but anyone taking away the shield
without possessing all these virtues would be totally dishon-
oured. If, though, he were fortunate enough to have these good
qualities and his sweetheart were as loyal as I've just explained,
then you may be certain that once he had slung it at his neck, all
his virtues would double: his heart, his strength and his might.'

– 'Indeed,' said Gawain, 'that shield has excellent properties.' –
'You are right,' said the girl. 'It has brought many knights to grief;
and I'm sure it will do the same to those who expect to be helped by
the goodness of their sweethearts – they may well be let down. I've
seen a hundred of them turn up, all on their own, wanting to carry
it off, because they thought they had paragons of mistresses so
devoted to their interests that they believed that with their encour-
agement they, and they alone, would surpass all others – kings,
counts, emperors, however rich in lands and honour. What stupid-
ity! Once they had grasped the shield's strap and fitted it to their
neck, their folly was plain to them for immediately they were
unhorsed and defeated. So in the end they declared that a man is
extremely foolish to so believe and trust in the love of a woman as
to undertake anything, however trivial, on her assurance. Thus
they lamented their great misfortune on their own account and
grieved all the more because my brother was small and yet had got
the better of them and thrown them to the ground; for the shield
would have been carried off but for his defence of it.' (C. II, § 29,
Mss ELMPQSTUV, ll. 29246–310, 29472–537)

Treachery at the ferry (3934 ff.)

*Perceval comes to a broad river, which he recognises as the one
where he had first met the Fisher King.*

He would have liked to cross that river and go to the king's court,
seeing how beautiful and well inhabited the countryside was on
the other side. So he then prayed God that he might find a way

over, either some ford or a bridge. With this in mind he rode on through the morning until after midday, when he saw a small castle splendidly situated on a hillside above the water. It had a central tower set within strong outer walls. Not finding anywhere to cross, Perceval kept riding on hard until he was soon directly opposite the castle. There he found some old entrenchments and beaten tracks. On he went deep in thought and came upon an old dwelling, a little castle in ruins, but with its gateway intact. When he reached the gate, he went through it to find a maiden sitting beneath an almond tree; and he saw she had a comb which she was passing through her hair.

On seeing him, she put down her comb and addressed him: 'So help me God, my good friend. I know you've been looking for a means to cross. And you are very welcome to have one, for you're a good knight.' Then she got up and led him outside. Perceval, very anxious to make the crossing, looked her up and down, but without caring to ask her about herself. Then they found a well harnessed mule, on which the extremely beautiful and attractive damsel mounted. She led him over to the bank, where she found a barge of hers. The mule, which was used to this, jumped in so that the whole barge rocked; and she said: 'In you get, good sir!' Perceval pulled his horse round; but it gave a start, neighed, snorted and bucked, unwilling to be forced aboard. The maiden called on him to get in; but he replied: 'By all the saints in the world, damsel, I'm quite unable to.' Just then, from the other direction, a boatman shouted to him at the top of his voice: 'Don't get in, sir knight, because she's certainly want-ing to drown you! That's her only occupation. If you'd gone on board, it would have been much the worse for you.'

My lords, it would take more than today to tell you of all the evil she perpetrated or how she deceived people, for you have never heard such a truly amazing thing since the day you were born. She persistently pressed Perceval hard to get in. Then, when she failed to trick him into it, she was very distressed. For his part, the man who was calling on him to flee did not neglect to come for him; and Perceval made the crossing with him. This boatman lost no time in telling him of that astonishing custom. (*C. II, § 3, Mss EPT*, ll. 20023–95)

The light from the castle (4058–95)

Gawain is on a mission and, having already ridden throughout one night, continues without pause the next day.

He entered a great forest, through which he went from morning until sunset, when he emerged onto a plain and saw the sea. His good mount headed rapidly in that direction. My lord Gawain had had no sleep the previous night and had passed a hard day; and, having been through wind and rain without food or drink, was exceptionally tired and drooping in the saddle, so desperate for sleep that he could scarcely hold himself up. With his horse pulling and tugging at the bridle, he relaxed his grip a little and let it have its head. It carried him on like this until, as night fell, he reached the sea. Unable to go any further, he was full of gloomy thoughts, when his horse made for a causeway it saw ahead stretching far out into the sea. As soon as it reached it, the good steed wanted to go along it.

The causeway, which was not broad, was planted on both sides with cypresses, pines and laurels. The branches of the trees joined to form a complete canopy over it. Bending down, my lord Gawain looked forward along it and saw in the far distance a light like a blazing fire. The horse wanted to go straight there; but he restrained it because of the raging sea, which was beating against the causeway as if to knock it to pieces and uproot all the trees, which were constantly clashing together with a dismal groaning as they were lashed by the gale. My lord Gawain was extremely afraid, and quite rightly, to go on it, vowing to wait for daylight before venturing there on any account. But the horse, I can tell you, pranced about and reared in such a violent manner that he was unable to calm it; and it wrenched the reins from his grasp. It took the bit so firmly between its teeth that, whether he liked it or not, it leapt ahead. And what did that good knight do? He let it go as it wished, surrendering the reins and bridle; and he kicked it hard and often with his spurs, sending it flying ahead. So he rode until midnight without ever coming to the source of the radiance. But on he travelled along the causeway until he arrived in a great hall. (*C. I, § V. 3, Mss TVD*, ll. 13083–42)

Gawain has come to the Grail Castle, where he is privileged to see the vessel and its associated marvels.

The lurking serpent (4210–317)

Gawain's adventures are interrupted by those of the knight Carados. After the latter has imprisoned his mother in a tower and humiliated her magician lover, they plot revenge by means of an enchanted serpent, which is shut in a cupboard in his mother's room.

Not long afterwards Carados thought he would like to go to see his mother in the tower. Alas, if only he knew the truth about the astonishing trick prepared for him by his mother! But he was unaware of it. Climbing quickly up in the tower, he came before the lady there and said: 'May the Saviour of the world who culls the wicked from the good preserve and bless you, my lady!' The queen's reply to this was quite different from what was in her heart: 'My dear, good son, may Jesus Christ keep you! I was not expecting you to come here so suddenly, for it's been some time since I saw you here. You've come upon me quite unawares and caught me with my hair down. My head was feeling rather uncomfortable, and I was wanting to attend to it with a comb brought from Caesarea; but it's in that cupboard over there. Would you be kind enough to bring it to me? Then stay and keep me company here, and we'll have a pleasant time: I love to have you with me, and it's very miserable for me always to be here on my own.'

Carados quickly jumped to his feet to do as she asked. He went over to the cupboard, then opened it and put his arm inside. At once the evil serpent darted at his arm and wrapped itself round it, attaching itself to it in a tight coil. Carados jumped backwards, confident of putting up a good defence against the serpent and its attack. He went to stretch his arm out, expecting to knock it off, but only to find it clinging more tightly and squeezing it all the harder. Then Carados began to turn pale and livid, to shake and tremble. At the top of his voice he called upon God on account of the agony he suffered. (C. I, § III. 11, Mss TVD, ll. 6303–52)

It is only much later that Carados is released from the serpent, which is decapitated.

The giant's castle (4460 ff.)

On his travels Perceval comes to a deep, rushing river.

Perceval looked across it and saw a very fine tower; but round it was neither wall nor moat, nor any hedge, palisade or enclosure. This put him in very good heart; and he said that if he were over there, he would have a lodging for the night; but he did not know how to cross. It then occurred to him to go downstream, and he would find some bridge or passage before he ever turned back. He then rode along the river, following its course; and looking ahead, he saw a very well-built stone bridge. Without pausing, he made straight for it and, having quickly galloped across, headed uphill. He did not stop before he had reached the tower, which was of excellent construction. There was a splendid tree, more handsome than he had ever seen, in front of the entrance; and he dismounted at once beneath that tree. He climbed up a flight of marble steps to the tower and went inside, to find the most beautiful residence ever seen by a Christian soul, the best furnished and decorated.

Perceval was not at all taken aback, but was delighted with his discovery. I might add that he saw not a soul, no knight, lady or servant, no living being from whom he could ask anything. Not knowing the place or the situation, he was unwilling to disarm. Set before a fine window he saw a silver table on which, it seems, there was a white cloth, salt, knives, beautiful, precious golden goblets, and such copious food as would have done full honour to a king. He saw too the water in two splendid, elegant basins, well crafted from pure gold; and the towel was not lacking, but was soft and white and finely woven.

Perceval was pleased with what he saw; and he felt great joy in his heart, as he was very tired and had not eaten for a considerable time. He quickly removed his armour and took a cloak of precious cloth from a stand in the hall, then went out of the door and down the staircase, relieved his horse of its bridle and left it to graze in peace, after which he returned. He went to one of the golden basins and took the water in it to wash, drying himself with the towel. Taking his seat in the very best position, he ate well to his satisfaction, for there was food in profusion: fresh meat, birds and venison, and a good supply of wine from which he drank as much as he wished. Thus he sat at his meal, completely alone, with no serving man or squire to speak to, and no company as he ate.

While he was occupied with his food, he glanced towards the door and saw a maiden appear who was in a wretched state: she was thin, and her complexion was colourless and sallow, yellowish and swarthy. To tell the truth, I suppose her dress was not worth twelve pence. Ill-clad as she was, she came before Perceval, greeted him, then said: 'Sir, so help me the Lord God, I'm very sad about that food, for which you'll pay so dear and which will bring you so much trouble.' – 'Fair one,' he replied, 'of whom, then, should I be worried or afraid?' – 'Indeed, sir, I don't want to hide it from you,' she said, and continued: 'The lord of this place is a giant, a very wicked, base creature, who had this tower built here. And no worthy man ever comes without being slain by him in his home.' – 'My friend,' said Perceval, 'that is indeed criminal wickedness. But tell me frankly if you don't belong to him yourself.' – 'No truly, sir,' she said; 'but he has kept me in his dwelling two full years and a half, to my great, heartfelt grief. I'm not prepared to submit to him, so he just treats me shamefully, allowing me neither to live nor to die; and I can't get free of him. But quick, don't delay: arm yourself instantly, because the giant will soon come back, and if he finds you in here, that will be the end of you!'

– 'My friend,' said Perceval, 'if it is really as you say, he'll not be able to get away scot free. If he wants to create trouble for me in here, I'll fight him first.' – 'Don't say that, good sir: it would be folly to fight, for he's immensely strong and huge, so that nobody at all could hold out against him. But arm yourself without delay and get out of this tower, to see if you're able to save yourself.' Perceval loses no time in arming, donning his hauberk, lacing his helmet and girding his sword. Then he vows to God who dwells on high that he will not leave his lodging, whatever anyone says to him, unless he is driven out by force.

He went to lean against the great, wide window. However, the giant, delighted to have spotted him, roared up at him: 'Who brought you here, vassal? You'll get good lodging tonight, but it will be to your misfortune.' Then, without stopping or saying another word, he advanced swiftly. He saw the horse and was enraged because it was grazing on the grass. With a club he was holding he dealt it a fantastic blow that shattered its back. At that Perceval was furious. He seized his shield and went down, thinking he would go mad with rage, and wishing to avenge his good horse slain by the giant.

The giant thought him quite stupid to come at him like this. In his fist he held his long, stout, solid club, which he heaved aloft with the intention of striking Perceval. He, however, made him miss by dodging to one side. From now on he had better look out, for if he can catch him with a blow, he will not have the chance to lament anyone else's grief. Perceval, very fearful of the club, grasped his naked sword and, without a challenge, struck a great blow at him, but without being able to measure it, as he was rather far away. He brought it down on his left side, striking his hip. Had the blow fallen straight, it would have severed the thigh; but the sword was deflected as it whistled down. It caught the thick part of the thigh so close to the bone that it sheared the heel clean off. The giant felt himself wounded and went so mad with anger and grief that his heart was near to bursting. He was distraught not to have killed him at the first attempt.

He put all his effort into a great assault, furiously bringing his club down with the aim of slaying him at a single stroke. The blow was brought violently down; but Perceval, a master at fencing, saw it coming and was not caught out. He jumped back, and the great stroke came crashing down so that the huge, massive club was shattered. Perceval was overjoyed and lost no time in assailing him with his sword. So viciously did he strike him that he sliced through his ear, severing it from his head, and clean through his shoulder and arm and into his side right to the lung. The giant fell unconscious. Then, without pausing, Perceval drove his good sword straight through his body. So he was slain: that was the end of it.

Perceval made his way back to the lodging, which he had well earned. With no one opposing his entry, in he went and quickly disarmed. There was no serving man or squire to give him any assistance, but just the girl, who graciously helped him with a will to the best of her ability. Her service was by no means unacceptable to Perceval: on the contrary, he appreciated and enjoyed it.

Unhesitatingly she said to him: 'Sir, now the house is yours, and you can do what you will in it. And I'm at your mercy; so in God's name have pity on me.' – 'Really, my friend,' said Perceval, 'you've no need to fear, for you'll not come to any harm at my hands. But tell me if you know whether there's a horse on the premises.' – 'Yes, indeed,' she said. 'There's a black one in the cellar over there. It must have been two months or more ago that the giant killed a very fine knight and put his charger in a big cellar down below. Then he kept it very well supplied with fodder and drink; and it's been there like that ever since.' Perceval heard this news with great satisfaction and pleasure. He asked for a candle, and she promptly brought him one that gave a good light; and then they went down to the cellar to look at the horse. As soon as he saw the steed, you may be sure he was delighted with it, and it appeared extremely fine and handsome. I am certain he would not have given it up for all the wealth in London town. Then they went back into the tower.

Perceval quickly went to bed stark naked, as he was extremely exhausted and the night pitch-black. He fell asleep totally fatigued; and the maiden went to bed in a panelled room. So they slept without any fear until dawn the next morning, when the sun rose brightly and filled the day with its light.

Perceval rose and dressed, very impatient to be staying there so long. He went to his horse and saddled it, with the maiden doing all she could to help him. He did not disdain, but much appreciated, her service. Yet he told her to stay behind and be mistress of the house and of all the surrounding countryside. She thanked him profusely, declaring that he had really been her saviour by rescuing her from the giant, who had so ill-treated her and slain many a good knight. 'That has greatly increased your renown, and may our Lord recompense you for it!' No more was said. Perceval armed, mounted his black steed, took his leave and then left at once and in haste, galloping away through the great, branching forest. (C. II, § 12, Mss *EKLMPQSTU*, ll. 21666–955)

The search for the hero (5384–411)

Over dinner King Arthur, sad at the absence of Perceval, hopes he may return safely to court.

Then Gawain responded. 'I shall certainly go to search for him,' he said, 'in however distant the land. And I shall leave early in the morning and never break my journey this side of the great

Dolorous Mount.' – 'And I shall go with you to look for Perceval,' said Yvain. 'And I'll not stop for more than a single night, if God preserves me from captivity, sickness and death, until I've been to that much famed Mount.'

More than thirty other knights pledge themselves to the quest, including Lancelot, Sagremor and Erec.

They all said they would go to look for Perceval and would not give up until they had found him. Having all taken this vow, they rose from their meal; and they went to take their ease in their lodgings until the morning. My lord Gawain finally took leave of the king his uncle and the bright-faced queen, who granted it reluctantly until he swore to them that he would return to court just as early as he could. So Gawain left them and, I believe, went to rest that night in his quarters until, at dawn next morning, he saw the sun flooding the whole world with light.

Then he quickly armed, mounted Gringalet with his shield at his neck and grasping his lance, and without further delay rode off out of the town. There he saw his companions awaiting him by a cross. They were armed and mounted on their brown, piebald, black or fallow horses, with the gold on their shields shining bright in the sunlight. That does not surprise me, for they were forty knights among the best in the world and armed to their liking. My lord Yvain, son of King Urien, who showed all the virtues, was the first to address my lord Gawain, placing his hand on his steed's mane. 'Sir,' he said, 'the knights would all have split up by now, but they weren't certain which way you wanted to go.' Gawain replied straight away that he is going to look for Perceval and, if God keeps him from harm, he will seek out the Fisher King, who once did him great honour. [*He explains at some length how he will go by way of the Grail Castle, hoping to learn its secrets.*]

When they had heard what he had to say, the companions went their different ways with all speed, each going in search of

adventure where he thought he might find it. Gawain then set off
into the great, leafy forest in the company of Yvain and Lancelot,
all three riding together through the woodland, I believe. They
emerged onto a vast, broad heath, through which there ran a fine
river, beautiful and clear. The three lords on their horses came
directly to the water; and as the river flowed very gently, it could
be crossed without a bridge. So, once their mounts had drunk,
the lords rode to the other side. Beneath a tall, leafy tree they
came across an old highway that forked into three wide roads, all
very broad but, I think, little frequented. Gawain was the first to
speak, saying to his companions: 'Sirs, this is where we separate,
and each should make his own way. Now I pray God to direct us
so that we find what we are seeking; and the first back to court
should wait there for his companions.' This was agreed by each
man, and they separated without further discussion. I have not
found in the story what became of my lord Yvain, nor of Lancelot,
who made straight along the broad road he took; and I shall not
tell of the adventures encountered by the others, nor will you
hear me speak of the roads and tracks they followed. I just want
to tell you what we learn of Gawain from the story. (C. II, § 28,
Mss *ELMPQSTUV*, ll. 29024–37, 29067–116, 29153–99)

The radiance in the forest (5768–80)

Perceval meets a maiden who spurns his company. He neverthe-
less follows her through a forest after nightfall, wondering why
she has forbidden him to ride with her.

While he was thinking about this, he spotted in the far distance a
radiance like a burning candle. Having noticed it, he watched it
carefully. But very soon it seemed to him as if there were five of
them burning brightly; and so great was their brilliance that he
had the impression that the whole vast forest had been kindled by
their light and was blazing all around: it was a veritable marvel.
Even more than this, he fancied that the flame, which was bright

red, reached up to the heavens. He took it into his head to speak to the maiden and ask her straight out the source of this great radiance that was visible to them from such a distance.

He called to the damsel: 'Please tell me,' he said, 'about this fire I've seen.' She replied not a word, being some way away; for she had already gone on and left him without more ado. Perceval was not angry, but rather smiled a little. He was not greatly perturbed and quite undismayed: on the contrary, he determined and vowed to go and reach that radiance and not let fear hold him back. He rode on hard, faster than before.

Now Perceval is caught in a violent tempest; and when it has abated, he can no longer see the radiance. Next day he catches up with the maiden and finds her more communicative. He asks if she too was surprised by the storm.

'No indeed, sir,' she said. 'I never even noticed any rain or gale. Quite the opposite: it was a really lovely night, quiet and calm and windless, as beautiful as I've ever seen in my life. As for the radiance you saw, I don't know if you've ever heard of the rich king who is a fisherman. He lives near here, on the other side of a river. Last night he slept out in the forest, as he very much likes to do. That's where the great radiance came from which you asked me about. And the fire that rose so high showed the presence of the Grail, which is so beautiful and precious and in which the glorious bright blood of the King of Kings was caught when he was hung on the cross: he had it with him in the woods, so that the devil wouldn't deceive anyone seeing it at that time, or set him on the evil path of committing any wicked crime. The king has the Grail carried with him because he is a holy, devoutly religious man, who leads a very fine life. To our Lord, who does not forget the worthy man who repents the wicked deeds of his youth, he often prays to take him to heaven under his protection and keep him from committing any treacherous sin.' (*C. II*, § 22, Mss *EKLMPQSTUV*, ll. 25608–43, 25777–811)

The tournament (6296 ff.)

Perceval is advised by Briol, a friendly castellan, that to achieve success at the court of the Fisher King he must first prove himself the best of knights. To this end he is directed to a great tournament in which King Arthur and his men will participate at the Proud Castle. Proceeding by way of a marvellous bridge and a vast forest, he arrives incognito before the castle and takes his stand among the Irish and Scots, the opponents of Arthur's party.

The battle lines are decided, the companies drawn up, and the fine steeds prance about. The banners wave in the wind, helmets sparkle and shields shine, and every man grasps his lance.

Then Kay dashed to the fore, requesting the joust; and King Arthur granted it to him to get the tournament under way. Without further ado or delay he advanced with a series of short bounds. Perceval recognised him clearly and charged against him, spurring his horse so that it flew along beneath him more quickly than a falcon swooping on a pigeon. Kay, for his part, came boldly at him. As the horses raced past, they struck each other on their blazoned shields. Kay at once snapped his lance in two so it did no further damage; but Perceval plunged his an arm's length through his shield, piercing and holing his good, finely meshed hauberk. As they came together, he struck him so hard that he toppled him to the ground over his steed's crupper. He took the horse and led it away. Kay had difficulty in getting up again, as he was slightly wounded.

Then came the general melee, and so hard was the clash that it made the earth shake. The king of Ireland, it seems, went to joust against Sagremor, piercing and bursting apart his gold-banded shield. Sagremor struck him in turn so that he lost both his stirrups and was brought to the ground. The Irish were there to get him back on his feet. Now the tourneying becomes fiercer, the jousting general, with knights bleeding as they wound and fell each other, striking with naked swords upon the steel helmets.

In it those notable for their deeds of arms performed marvellous handiwork. Gawain acted like Gawain and captured the king of Scotland, who was highly renowned in arms. And for the other side there was Perceval dealing out with his sword great, weighty blows in good measure: the Scots and Irish had a splendid companion in him. That Welshman ranged through the tourney with his burnished steel sword in his fist, intent not on booty but on performing knightly feats. The skirmishing, the pursuits and the melees continued until well into the evening. Then the combatants separated and dispersed.

Perceval leaves by the way he had come and spends the night with Briol in a remote hermitage. Arthur, meanwhile, enters the Proud Castle with his company.

They were quick to take off their armour and don costly robes before making their way into the hall. The mighty king went to Kay to see if he was injured at all; and he summoned all his doctors, who told him there was nothing serious. The knights laughed heartily at the seneschal behind his back because in the first joust he was unhorsed in full view of a thousand knights or more. The king himself joked about it, then asked the company if they knew the knight responsible. They said they had no idea who he was and had not recognised him by his shield. 'Certainly,' said my lord Gawain, 'I'm quite convinced he is extremely valiant and gallant and has surpassed us all to carry off this evening's prize.' Then the horn was sounded for the water, and the king washed and took his place at table; after him all the noble knights sat down to a meal of which I would have great trouble and difficulty in describing all the dishes.

I would like to tell you of those outside the castle, the Scots and the Irish bivouacked on the heath, and many another noble lord who had enquired and hunted everywhere to see if they could find the knight they had seen that evening. But however much they asked, they could not discover him or any

information about him, though with one accord they agreed that
he had won the prize in the face of them all. They spent the
whole night talking in this way in very high spirits until morning,
when the sun rose bright and beautiful.

Those outside and inside the castle got ready and had a
meal of bread and wine. Without more ado the good steeds
were promptly made ready and draped in their identification
markings; and the pennons were bound to the smooth ash
shafts of the lances. The knights lost no time in putting on
their iron greaves, lacing up their knee-pieces and donning
their shining hauberks. Both outside and inside, the men
armed, then assembled on the field. That was the most splendid plain anyone had ever seen, covered with lush, green grass
and excellent for tourneying. There you might have seen many
a fine charger in their assorted caparisons; and there were so
many lances and banners that it was wonderful to behold.
There was such a host of bucklers in vermilion, gold, red and
silver that the whole countryside shone with them. On both
sides the ranks were formed and drawn up in order, and it only
remained for them to join battle.

My lord Perceval had been travelling ever since daybreak and
had made such good time that he had already arrived at the tourney. However, he was not recognised, as he had left his arms with
Briol, who had supplied him with his own excellent set. That is
why those who were on the look-out and would have dearly
liked, on account of his prowess, to know his land of origin
failed to recognise him.

The tourneying got under way. If anyone then had cared to
watch the jousts, individual and general clashes, and mighty
sword-blows struck on gleaming steel helmets, he might well
have declared for sure that never in this world had such fierce
tourneying taken place along a single front on one stretch of
ground, except in mortal war. Nor would knights have borne
as much as they suffered as they strove not for booty but to
perform excellently.

I should like to tell you of King Arthur and how on the heath, between two ranks, he toppled the king of Ireland. He took his charger, a Spanish bay, and gave it to Sagremor, instructing him to return it to the king. What a sight to see were the knights of King Arthur's party, dealing blows at full stretch, breaking lances, piercing shields amid the clangour of ringing helmets! Those from outside mounted a good attack on them. Brian of the Isles did well, whilst the king of Scotland and his men performed with great credit. The king of Ireland was remounted among his men, whom he then exhorted to deeds of chivalry, which each of them agreed and promised him to do.

And what should I tell you of Perceval and the marvels he personally achieved? He brought the king's nephew Gueheret down from his Gascon horse in full view of the Bretons. Then Gawain came on the scene with Lancelot and my lord Yvain, causing a tremor throughout the ranks. There you could have seen blows meted out on helmets and gilded shields! Gallant, prudent Perceval held in his grasp his steel sword: he would make them quit the field or else would have a poor opinion of himself. He spurred his good steed and plunged into the thickest of the press, where he felled two of their most illustrious knights, companions of Gawain: one was noble Lancelot, the other the haughty Agravain. Then he struck to right and left, and it could well be said that the master of all knights had arrived: he was very soon recognised as such, I think, as he should have been. He went ceaselessly backwards and forwards, charging through the press and often making them give ground. Through his efforts the Irish rallied.

The courtly king of Scotland jousted with my lord Yvain. They broke their lances at the first shock, but did not fall from their horses or follow up their attack. On all sides the tourney was under way. King Arthur stayed on horseback outside it in order to watch Sir Perceval, whom he did not recognise; and he saw him rein in his steed quite still in the middle of the throng. Then he watched him strike and pursue all the best of his company, observing that none of them prevented him from doing just as he wished. Next he saw him hacking his way through the press, his naked sword in his hand, and then that the party from outside were all rescued by his efforts alone. He watched him demonstrating his prowess that the whole world should prize, and saw that had he set his mind on taking any spoils, he would have been able to have his pick of horses and knights themselves. So bold and proud was he that he feared no mother's son. For the whole day Brian of the Isles and his troop were with him and found in him a fine friend and a stout wall and fortress. If they maintain their prowess, their winnings from the tournament will be a good thousand silver marks.

When the king had watched all this, he called Gawain across. 'Nephew,' he said, 'you can see a splendid knight on that black steed: I've never seen his like in all my life. God bless me, dear nephew, do enquire and find out his name and his land at the end of today's proceedings; and tell him straight to come to me, as I summon him. And if he were willing from now on to be a member of my household in your company, I would cherish him more than any living soul. He has struck so many sword-blows today that it quite amazes me; and still he strikes on just as he began.' – 'Sire, so help me the Holy Cross,' replied my lord Gawain, 'it's my firm opinion and impression that he is the best in the world.'

With that they both entered the tournament together, where they dealt many a lusty blow and made those from outside give ground. Now Gawain showed all his dashing valour and chivalry. The great throng assembled by the king of Scotland was now broken up and would have been on the retreat, when the king of Ireland came on the scene. The king of Scotland was brought down, then rescued and remounted; and the pursuit was halted. It was by then almost midday. King Arthur and his company struck many a stout blow. Those from outside held out like worthy, valiant men; and by the help of Perceval, who was completely unknown to them, they made a fine stand that day.

Then, greatly fatigued, they dispersed and left to go to their quarters and rest. King Arthur renewed his appeal to Gawain to go in search of the stranger knight, and he was very happy to do so. He went among the knights asking for the one he will not find, because he had gone back through the forest, riding at full speed. So when my lord Gawain saw that he would not find him, he went to tell the king, explaining that, despite searching high and low, he had been unable to find the knight or hear any news of him. They let the matter rest at that, but continued to sing his praises.

The men outside also went to look for him and made enquiries throughout the castle. Brian of the Isles was far from pleased that he had slipped off in this way. For a long time they searched and sought news of him, but were unable to glean any information at all. (C. II, § 24, Mss *EKLMPQSTUV*, ll. 26865–931, 26969–7219)

Perceval had returned through the forest to be met by Briol, from whom he received further hospitality before resuming his adventures.

APPENDIX B

Guillaume le Clerc: William Malveisin[1]

Whereas in previous studies I have insisted that Guillaume le Clerc could have composed his romance without ever having set foot in Scotland, the discovery of a historical Galiena (by no means a common name) now inclines me to the view that he is more likely to have spent at least some time in the country. The situation in brief is that we find in *Fergus* a basically sound knowledge of Scottish topography, especially of the region south of the Forth known as Lothian, the heartland of the romance being Melrose, Roxburgh and Jedburgh; and one also encounters the names of certain historical figures from the past (St Mungo or Kentigern, Somerled and Fergus himself) and now, it seems, a contemporary personage, Galiena, who provided Guillaume with the name of his heroine. This assumption rests not only on the nominal identity of the two ladies, but also on their family connections with the lordship of Lothian.[2]

Galiena's ancestor, Cospatric, had been made earl of Northumberland by William the Conqueror, and his son, Cospatric II, was the first earl of Dunbar and of Lothian. The latter's nephew, of the same name, possessed lands on the north and south shores of the Forth and was, with the abbot of Dunfermline, 'lord of the ferries' at the crossing point known today as Queensferry. His lands and rights were apparently inherited by his son, Waltheof, who was dead by 1200. Galiena was one of Waltheof's two daughters. In a number of documents of the early 1200s she appears as the wife of Philip de Mowbray, who in about 1211 was constable of Edinburgh and had become a staunch intimate and counsellor to King William the Lion. Her relations in the parallel branch of the family still styled them- selves lords of Lothian.

There is no way of dating *Fergus*, but its extensive use of the First and Second Continuations of the *Perceval* suggests the last decade of the twelfth century as the earliest possible time of composition. If therefore we are looking for an author resi- dent in Scotland, it is most reasonable to keep our eyes open for any French clerk by the name of William (Guillaume) prac- tising at this period, and preferably having connections with Lothian and moving in much the same circles as Galiena and her husband. His French nationality presents no problem: as witness the lament of one early thirteenth-century writer, 'The modern kings of Scotland count themselves as Frenchmen in race, manners, language and culture; they keep only Frenchmen in their household and following and have reduced the Scots to utter servitude.'[3] The name William, however, is unfortunately common, and a brief search of the records soon turns up two or three possible candidates. Yet there is one in particular who demands our attention: a certain William Malveisin (or Malvoisin, a modernised form), whom we first meet as a royal clerk witnessing documents concerning lands in Lothian, issued in one case at Kinghorn on the north shore of the Forth. He is, we assume, a young man, but on the verge of an illustri- ous career.[4]

He most probably hailed from a family of the lower Seine valley and came to Scotland equipped with some legal training, possibly acquired in Paris or Rheims, where the twelfth-century Archbishop Samson may have been his uncle.[5] Arriving in Scotland apparently in the mid-1180s, he became by 1193 arch- deacon of Lothian and, in a swift progression, bishop of Glasgow in 1200, having been consecrated priest at Lyons, and then in 1202 bishop of St Andrews, an office he held until his death in

1238. As well as his journey to France for his consecration in 1200, we know of two or three other occasions when he returned to the Continent: twice on extended visits to the papal court and once perhaps to visit relatives in France.

Of any literary activity on his part we have no proof, although he has been credited with works now lost on Saint Ninian and Saint Kentigern or Mungo. Even if this attribution is correct, a pious Latin treatise is a far cry from our romance. On the other hand, a recent biographer has found little religiosity in his character.[6] So it is by no means impossible that at some stage in his career he indulged a taste for vernacular composition. A generation later perhaps, the bishop of Lincoln, Robert Grosseteste, wrote works in French verse, though in more moralistic vein. For in *Fergus* I detect no very serious purpose, but believe it to be essentially a playful travesty of certain fashionable literary texts, incorporating some non-fictional elements in the shape of historical characters and, conceivably, events. Let us see what Malveisin's own experience could have contributed to the romance.

First there is the surprisingly accurate knowledge, so often noted, of Scottish geography. Of the places named in the text, we have documentary proof of Malveisin's close association with or, at one time or another, presence in Glasgow, Edinburgh, Dunfermline, Queensferry, Melrose, Roxburgh and Jedburgh; moreover, as Bishop of St Andrews his see incorporated the region of Lothian. The relative vagueness of the presentation of Galloway could be due to a lack of first-hand knowledge of that notoriously unruly territory. Dunnottar he would almost certainly have known, situated as it was on the well-travelled road between Arbroath and Aberdeen, but the story required it to be a remote and mysterious place.

When we turn to the characters there are some surprises in store. There is no question of Malveisin having known the historical Fergus, lord of Galloway: he had died in 1161, ending his days, interestingly enough, not in his home territory but as an

Augustinian canon in Holyrood Abbey. Although his son Uhtred
had been murdered by his brother in 1174, Uhtred's son Roland
(who died in 1200) and grandson Alan were very much in evidence
in Malveisin's day. A *protégé* of King William, Roland was justi-
ciar of Galloway and in 1196 received the important royal office
of constable, which passed to Alan after his death.

Another prominent figure known to Malveisin was Ranulf de
Soules, lord of Liddesdale. His uncle, a Norman baron of the
same name from Northamptonshire, had been granted the lands
of Liddesdale and there built Liddel Castle. He became the royal
butler, an office inherited by his nephew. The latter, who seems to
have been a rather troublesome character, is said to have been
killed in the castle in 1207 by his domestics.

Galiena de Mowbray, the grandson and great-grandson of
Fergus (themselves lords of Galloway), the castellan of Liddel:
Malveisin not only knew of these people, but had direct contact
with them, as appears in various royal charters and other documents of the period. In Edinburgh in 1194, for instance, as
archdeacon of Lothian he witnessed an agreement between St
Andrews and Durham together with Roland of Galloway and
Ranulf de Soules. In 1199 as bishop-elect of Glasgow and royal
chancellor his name appears as witness before that of Alan of
Galloway; and as Bishop of St Andrews in about 1210 he is
similarly associated with Alan and with Philip de Mowbray, that
is with the great-grandson of Fergus and the husband of Galiena.
Other collocations of these names could be quoted, and that
of Galiena herself appears, linked with her husband's, in
Dunfermline records when, in 1212, a dispute between them and
the abbey was adjudicated by Malveisin in the presence of
Queen Ermengarde and various other prelates. One unnamed
character in the romance who nevertheless plays a significant
role by sponsoring Fergus at Arthur's court is the royal chamberlain. William the Lion was served in this capacity by Philip
de Valognes, and he too appears as co-witness with Malveisin to
various charters, including those of 1199 and 1210 just

mentioned. It is clear that William Malveisin could not have been better placed or informed, should he have wished to compose, as a relaxation from his clerical duties, a light-hearted pastiche incorporating some elements of a *roman à clef*. This encourages us to see if there are other features of the romance that could support a possible ascription to him.

In an earlier study, I gave as follows my impression of the author of *Fergus*: 'Guillaume le Clerc I see above all as a literary man with literary interests, a poet who freely followed his own talents without needing to harness them to the requirements of a patron or wishing to use them in the promotion of any social or political cause. He was no moraliser. [. . .] From his lines a quite distinct personality emerges. Paradoxically for a dealer in the fantastic, he was a realist with a legalistic streak that makes sporadic appearances; intelligent and sharp-witted; more conservative than reformist as regards the chivalric function and code of conduct.'[7] Marinell Ash could have been speaking of the same man in her assessment of Malveisin's personality: 'The impression which emerges of the man and his career is that of a well-trained and thorough man of ability, motivated not so much by religious feeling as by a desire for order and the restoration and maintenance of his position and rights.'[8] Malveisin certainly had 'a legalistic streak', to the extent that after his death his expertise in the law was noted by a prominent ecclesiastical judge. And in disputes, we can well imagine him vying with Fergus' own verbal belligerence. 'In his acts within his own diocese,' we are told, 'he was clearly energetic in asserting his episcopal rights, in recovering possessions which had been alienated by his predecessors, in containing the privileged position won by the monasteries in recent years by working for definitions of doubtful matters within the canon law [. . .]; this can hardly have made him popular in the monasteries of his diocese – he was remembered as harshly unfair in Dunfermline/ Inchcolm tradition [. . .] and as a "bad neighbour in every way" at Melrose.'[9]

If Malveisin was our poet, Fergus' adventure at the Queensferry crossing might well have had some basis in reality. Disputes over the ferry toll doubtless occurred. Galiena's grandfather had received a royal command to permit the passage of the Bishop of St Andrews and his men free of charge;[10] and a royal charter of about 1166 stipulated the same for those in the king's service. The puzzling reference to the 'castiel sarrasin' of Dunfermline (*Fergus*, ll. 4051–2) where Fergus is cast ashore may have something to do with the fact that it declined somewhat under William the Lion as a royal centre. It could on the other hand suggest strained relations between the poet and the local inhabitants, a situation not unknown to Malveisin, as during the abbacy at Dunfermline of Patrick (1202–1217): 'It was during his tenure of office that Bishop Malvoisin of St Andrews deprived the Abbey of its right of presentation to the churches of Hailes and Kinglassie because, on the occasion of a visit to Dunfermline, the abbot and monks had failed to provide him with sufficient wine for his evening collation. The defence was that the wine had been consumed by the bishop's own attendants.'[11]

If Malveisin was prepared to make an issue of the proper provision of food and drink to which he felt entitled, so was the Fergus of romance. In his famished state, he claimed from the band of robbers he encountered his right to a good meal for appropriate payment (ll. 3342 ff.). Later he made the supply of eels for the royal table a subject for banter at the expense of the upended Kay (ll. 6461 ff.); and it is interesting to find in one of King William's acts Dunfermline Abbey confirmed in the annual receipt of a tithe of the royal eels supplied by a subject in Fife, an area, it seems, especially rich in the commodity.[12] If gastronomic details would not appear out of place in a text by Malveisin, nor would the complimentary description of the merchant who gave Fergus passage back to Queensferry (ll. 4360 ff.), since we know that he had twice sponsored merchants from France.[13]

From the dry bones of the surviving documents one cannot, of course, tell whether Malveisin had a particular taste for the chivalric romance so much in vogue in his day. King William was certainly greatly influenced by the current ideals of knightly behaviour, which must have been encouraged in his entourage. In the romance, the main location of King Arthur's court in Carlisle was primarily determined by the parodying of the beginning of Chrétien's *Yvain*; but the memory of the knighting there in 1149 of the future King Henry II by his great-uncle David, King of Scots, may have partly inspired that of Fergus by Arthur. It is possible that Malveisin visited Carlisle with King William when, in 1186, he met Henry II there with the purpose of bringing Roland of Galloway to heel. It is perhaps significant that in the romance Fergus was prepared for his knighting by the courtly chamberlain (ll. 1110 ff.); for along with William the Lion, only his chamberlain, Philip de Valognes, is on record as distinguishing himself in the chivalric joust,[14] an exercise in which Fergus was to show himself the supreme master in the tournament at Jedburgh.

It was, however, at Roxburgh that Fergus performed his finest feats of arms. The castle there was one of King William's chief strongholds except during the disastrous years from 1174 to 1189 when, following William's capture at Alnwick and the Treaty of Falaise, Henry II maintained a garrison of English troops there and at Edinburgh. It is tempting to see in the romance a distortion of this historical fact in the extended siege of Roxburgh by an unnamed king who has laid claim to Galiene's land. William's surrender of the stronghold took place in the context of his attempt to recover his lost territories in northern England. Malveisin was, of course, thoroughly familiar with the situation and also, one assumes, with the king's earlier rash offer, reported by Jordan Fantosme,[15] to stake his claim on the result of a single combat between individual knights. That strikingly parallels the solution proposed by Galiene in her own desperate plight (ll. 5258 ff.).

The romance ends happily with King Arthur, in conformity with Scottish practice, bestowing Galiene on Fergus in marriage.

This took place in Roxburgh where, in 1193, William the Lion gave his natural daughter in marriage to Eustace de Vesci. As archdeacon of Lothian at the time, Malveisin may have been present at the ceremony, though Roxburgh itself lay in the Glasgow diocese.

Places, people, events: so much in the romance synchronises with what we can know of Malveisin's activities, experience, even his personality. Was he, then, its author? If so, when and where did he compose it? The case must rest in anticipation of the good Scottish verdict of 'not proven'. Yet William Malveisin does fit more snugly than any previous contender into the role of Guillaume le Clerc.

Notes to Appendix B

1 This Appendix contains the gist of a more detailed study currently in preparation. I am indebted to Miss Linda M. Gowans for bringing to my attention the historical prototype for the romance's heroine and so initiating this new line of enquiry.

2 My main sources of information for genealogies, documentation and historical background are, except when otherwise stated: Sir James Balfour Paul (ed.), *The Scots Peerage*; G. W. S. Barrow (ed.), *The Acts of William I*; and G. W. S. Barrow, *The Anglo-Norman Era in Scottish History*.

3 Barrow, *The Acts of William I*, p. 5.

4 See especially the detailed biography by D. E. R. Watt in his *Biographical Dictionary of Scottish Graduates to A.D. 1410*, pp. 374–9.

5 Marinell Ash, *The Administration of the Diocese of St Andrews 1202–1328*, pp. 392–3.

6 Ash, p. 4 (see below).

7 D. D. R. Owen, 'The Craft of Guillaume le Clerc's *Fergus*', p. 79.

8 Ash, p. 4.

9 Watt, p. 378.

10 Paul, vol. III, p. 244.

11 J. M. Webster, *Dunfermline Abbey*, p. 19.

12 Barrow, *The Acts of William I*, p. 195.

13 Watt, p. 376.

14 R. L. Graeme Ritchie, *The Normans in Scotland*, pp. 358–9.

15 *Jordan Fantosme's Chronicle*, ed. Johnston, ll. 334–7.